HEALING DECREES *THAT ACTIVATE* ANGEL ARMIES

Destiny Image Books by Tim Sheets

Healing Decrees That Activate Angel Armies

Angel Armies: God's Supernatural Enforcers

Prayers and Decrees That Activate Angel Armies

Angel Armies on Assignment

The New Era of Glory: Stepping Into God's Accelerated Season of Outpouring and Breakthrough

Planting the Heavens

Angel Armies: Releasing the Warriors of Heaven

Heaven Made Real: A Biblical Guide to the Afterlife and Eternity

God's Got This: Power Decrees (with Rachel Shafer)

Come Home: Pray, Prophesy & Proclaim God's Promises Over Your Prodigal (with Rachel Shafer)

HEALING DECREES THAT ACTIVATE ANGEL ARMIES

Partnering with Heaven's Supernatural Enforcers to Release Miracles, Signs, and Wonders

TIM SHEETS

DESTINY IMAGE® PUBLISHERS, INC.
P.O. Box 310, Shippensburg, PA 17257-0310
"Publishing cutting-edge prophetic resources to supernaturally empower the body of Christ"

This book and all other Destiny Image and Destiny Image Fiction books are available at Christian bookstores and distributors worldwide.

For more information on foreign distributors, call 717-532-3040.
Reach us on the Internet: www.destinyimage.com.

ISBN 13 TP: 979-8-8815-0640-7
ISBN 13 EBook: 979-8-8815-0641-4

For Worldwide Distribution, Printed in the U.S.A.
1 2 3 4 5 6 7 8 / 30 29 28 27 26

Dedication

To our children and grandchildren: Rachel (Mark) and Madeline, Lily, Jude, and Jaidin, and Joshua (Jessica), Joelle, Sam, Grace, and Caroline: may you always use His Word to decree His Kingdom come, and angel army assistance to see it established. Never forget... God never lies, because of Him, we win!

Contents

1

Reality Church

We decree we have stepped into God's accelerated season of outpouring and breakthrough.

A tremendous move of Christ's Kingdom is beginning on the earth. Something huge is taking place. Long-awaited promises, cries of the heart, are beginning to happen in our times. The prophets are describing it as a new era. The word *era* means a new period of history. New years begin that are different from past years. It is a clear new period of times on the earth. Something is beginning that is going to be unlike anything we have experienced in the past. It is not vague; it is not blurry; it is clear. A magnificent new era is now due to activate in Christ's Kingdom. It is potent with Holy Spirit power, waiting for the saints to engage.

Our world has entered a defining moment. It is a tipping-point moment wherein we reap what we have sown. Tipping-point moments, or defining moments, are decided by who defines the moment. King Jesus has called His Ekklesia, His ruling and reigning body, His governing intercessors to rise up and define this moment. We have been prepared and He expects us to do it. We have been prepared by the prayers of millions of intercessors crying out to God, by the awesome Holy Spirit who is our Teacher and our Empowerer. We have been prepared by the revelation of the apostles and prophets. We have been prepared by prophetic dreams as well as the activation and assistance of Angel Armies under Holy Spirit supervision. We have been prepared by thousands of prophetic words, visions, signs, and wonders.

No other period of time in church history is comparable to the age we have now entered. We will see each of the anointings Holy Spirit poured out over the past 2,000 years released again in this new era simultaneously. We will see the ages converge and all of the different streams birthed by Holy Spirit merge together and flow in an unstoppable mighty river throughout the earth. Productivity and function will synergize, led by Holy Spirit. The Church will now implement new strategies, soaked in wisdom and experience and bathed in prayer and His presence. There's never been an era like this one.

The righteous remnant will begin to function as true heirs with Christ. This era will be marked by supernatural signs, wonders, healings, and miracles that will be visibly seen, and even media outlets will report what was once thought to be impossible has now happened.

In this new era King Jesus will make His stand alongside His people in very clear and powerful ways. Indeed, He will fulfill the prophetic word of Micah 2:13 (paraphrased), *"Messiah, the Breaker, will go before them, and they will break through."* We are entering days of supernatural breakthrough. It is not off in the distance; it is here and we are seeing it unfold now.

Along with the King making His stand, we will see, as well, that a true New Testament Church will make her stand. The Ekklesia and genuine governing authority will be seen on the earth. The days of pretend Christianity are over. It is a new day. It's a new era. It is time for reality church!

Prayer

Father, I bless Your Ekklesia, Your Church. I bless her to be all You called her to be, filled with a fresh anointing of Your Spirit, led by Your heart. Give us great boldness to do all You have appointed us to do in this hour.

2
Word Seeds

We decree our words are "lifed" with the power of the Holy Spirit.

We are told that God planted the heavens and the earth with word seeds—words that became what He decreed. Heaven and earth became what He seeded, decreed, and described with His words. From the beginning God was sharing with man, who was made in His image and likeness, how they could partner with Him and be creators by decreeing word seeds. We do not create from nothing like God did, but we take what God has done and steward it in such a way that we can decree a creative force into the heavens and the earth.

We can also create gardens like Eden, filled with fruit and abundance—gardens in the natural realm and the spirit realm. We can plant words filled with life—words that when believed, decreed, and acted upon become the very thing they describe. Word seeds have the innate ability to become what they are describing. They are seeds releasing their inner codes to reproduce in the soil in which they are planted.

Words are very powerful. They effect change. They loose power. They release potential. They instruct. They release strategies that can be acted upon. God shows from the very beginning the vital importance and power of words. Nothing activates the Kingdom of God and the Angel Armies like the Word of God. Holy Spirit hovers until He hears the Word of God. God's Word activates His power and Kingdom resources.

Psalm 103:20 says that *angels hearken* to the voice of God's Word. The entire universe is made to respond to the voice of God's Word. The heavens and the earth are made to respond to the powerful voice of His Word. Amazingly, human beings made in His image and in His likeness are carriers of that Word when they are activated at the new birth. They are "lifed" by it when they are born again.

God's Word also opens creative spheres, releasing creativity and creative abilities. Genesis 1:2 (NKJV) says, *"The earth was without form, and void; and darkness was upon the face of the deep. And the Spirit of God was hovering over the face of the waters."* The earth was without shape, in utter chaos, and it was nonproductive. It was a barren place until God's Word came forth. Notice that the condition of the heavens and the earth were dependent on the Word of God. Its productivity was dependent on the Word of God, and it still is to this day. The answer to chaos, disorder, barrenness, and darkness is the declared Word of God. The seeds of change are in the Word itself.

What possibilities has God given to man? What opportunities has He given us when we understand the principle that words are seeds? Plant words of life. Plant them in the heavens. Plant them on the earth. Plant them in your life, business, and children. Plant purpose-filled seeds.

PRAYER

Father, You have made us to be Your image bearers in word and action. I pray as the psalmist did, "May the words of my mouth be pleasing to You." May the words of my mouth activate the plans and purposes of Your heart and the Kingdom of Heaven come to earth through the word seeds I plant!

3

Miracles That Speak

We decree there is no king like our King. There is no god like our God.

Jesus is stepping to center stage with His Ekklesia to reveal He is miraculous in power. He still does creative miracles. The world is going to see and will say, *"There is no king like our King. There is no god like our God."* Scriptures are going to make history declaring His miraculous power. Notable miracles that we've preached are coming. Cripples are going to run, just as the crippled man did in Acts 3 at the temple gate. Blind eyes are going to open. The King is going to work through us. He is the same yesterday, today, forever. Deaf ears are going to hear, dramatic healings will be seen, cancer is going to dissolve.

Miracles will breathe life into prodigals. Miracles will declare Jesus is Lord. Miracles will declare there is no kingdom on the earth like our Kingdom.

The King says to His Church through Holy Spirit:

> "I will step forward as Lord of Hosts, mighty and strong in battle. For the challenge of hell and this world will not go unchallenged.
>
> "Move forward in the shaking that is now accelerating, says the Lord. Move forward. Move forward as the shaking time covers your advancement into new positioning. It covers it, hides it. Move forward as gross darkness blinds the enemies of My Kingdom from seeing the devastating traps I have put in their

paths. Move forward as My angels implement ruses and plans that draw the attention of the wicked and their resources and cause them to move in directions resulting from their devilish wisdom in greater and greater and greater numbers, for I am now gathering the vultures. My victory plans are not the defeat of a few. It is a defeat of the many.

"Move forward, Ekklesia, as My plans unfold. Move forward, sons and daughters, into new authority, power, and spiritual weapons that are mighty and stronghold destroying. Move forward as angel forces are positioning with you for supernatural victories. Move forward under the canopy of My presence, My protective hands, and My arms of strength. Move forward as My Kingdom aligns for the new time.

"Oppressive bands of wickedness will be broken. The Lord says, trust Me and you will one day proclaim: There have been battles. There have been perils. We have learned great lessons.

"There has been wilderness. There has been drought. There has been persecution. It has not been easy. There have been testings. There has been tribulation, but the overwhelming goodness of the Lord has brought us through. The overwhelming kindness of our God never failed us and we possess the land.

"It was little by little but our God rose on our behalf and broke the back of our oppressors. Our God has provided miracles of breakthrough. You will say miracles have brought us through oceans, fires, and floods."

PRAYER

King Jesus, we decree and believe that You are establishing Yourself as Lord of Hosts in our midst. We make way for You to come and Your Kingdom to reign here on earth!

4

Ask for Rain

We decree the release of healing rains right now.

Now is the time. Holy Spirit is saying, *Move forward in this supernatural age*. He's calling us, the King's Ekklesia, to stretch our faith now to believe for miracles. Undeniable miracles will spring forth in our midst. The harvest of Father's house will be seen gathering in, as a result of the miracles, signs, and wonders that are seen, that are evident and clear and validate Jesus is real.

> "For the Lord of Hosts decrees, the loosing of My Ekklesia includes the loosing of My miracles. My Church will proclaim, 'Miracles be loosed,' and they will loose. Long-awaited miracles are loosed among us. Notable miracles, My Church will say, notable miracles are loosed in our midst. Ekklesia, believe Me for notable miracles. Believe Me and live in them. Believe Me and live in new inheritance. Command, command in My name. Command them to come. They are in their moment. Command them to come. They are in their moment.
>
> I will move in strength, positioning Myself for aggressive movement on the earth. You will see My strong arm as you've never seen it before. The world will see My aggressive nature. I do not bluff. I will show My greatness. I will reveal I have no rivals. I will display unmatched authority, revealing the weakness of those who resist Me. I will release strategies upon the earth to block the strategies of My adversaries, and it will be said by

your adversaries, 'What is blocking our strategies? Why won't this work?'

"I have seen them, says the Lord. I know them, and I will block, and I will destroy them. I will partner with My Church, releasing great wisdom. Great deliverance will reveal great freedom. I will move on My people's behalf in ways that will amaze, confound, and will dismay their foes. You will see the mighty hand of your God. You will see it in your personal lives. You will see it in your families. You will see it in your churches. You will see it in your nations. You will see it in the world."

Ask, ask for Holy Spirit rains. That's what the Scripture says. Ask for rain when it's time for rain. Ask for it. Ask for Holy Spirit rains.

"It's time for the healing rains, says the Lord. Pray them into this time. With decrees, command miracles to begin to accelerate in your midst. Use your authority and loose miracles. Agree with Heaven's plan. Loose miracles. Loose angels to assist the releasing of notable miracles with words of faith aligned with what I promise. Loose long-awaited miracles, says the Lord.

"The due seasons of promised signs, wonders, and miracles is now moving into Kingdom hubs. Exercise your authority in My Name and loose them into the earth realms or the earth realm of your region. For miracles will surely change history as in the Acts of the Apostles. For it is time for another Acts of the Apostles. This time, not twelve; this time, thousands. It's time for another Acts of the Apostolates.

"In My true Ekklesia—this time not just one in Jerusalem, but in hundreds around the world—miracles will be seen, validating, confirming: I am on your side."

PRAYER

Lord Jesus, we ask for the Holy Spirit rains to come and come now! May Your Spirit sweep across our lands, bringing refreshment, revival, and revealing You as the one true King!

5

THE LANGUAGE OF KINGS

We decree Your Kingdom is coming and coming and coming.

We are in a season when clearly we need to *do* the Word of God. The world is divided and crumbling because the Church and millions of Christians are not doing their assignment. The world that most of us knew growing up is coming apart at the seams because much of the Church has not been doing what God says. We have to be doers of the Word of God. Allow the Holy Spirit to activate this in you.

Job 22:28 (KJV) says, *"Thou shalt also decree a thing, and it shall be established unto thee: and the light shall shine upon thy ways."*

The Amplified Bible of Job 22:28 reads: *"You will also decide and decree a thing, and it will be established for you; and the light [of God's favor] will shine upon your ways."*

Favor and decrees of faith go hand in hand. Alexander Douay's translation of the Hebrew to English says, *"Thou shalt decree a thing, and it shall come to thee, and light shall shine on thy ways."* That is an excellent translation of the Hebrew language. Decree something and it will come to you. You will pronounce something to be, and God will make it so. That, of course, refers to authority language—the language of kings.

The word for *decree* is the Hebrew word *gazar,* and it means to decide and to purpose. It is also used 11 times in the Hebrew Old Testament meaning "to divide, to sever, or to cut off" (Strong's

H1504). For example, *gazar* is the word used at the Red Sea. It says the Red Sea was cut off. Moses stood in front of the Red Sea and he spoke with authority. He used kingly language and put the Dominion Mandate into an activated form, a bold command. He raised the rod of authority and he spoke kingly language. He spoke words of ruling authority and he literally said to the sea, "Separate. Open. Divide." Sounds similar to what our King says in Matthew 16:18. You have been given authority to declare things to open or to close. Open things with your decrees.

Moses says that what you purpose you must put into words of command, decree them, speak them, and they will be established unto you. Speak like a king in the King's lineage. Speak like you are a joint heir with King Jesus. Speak with the authority Jesus gave us in His Name. Come into an alignment with the Dominion Mandate of God in Genesis from the beginning. In other words, in Jesus' Name *gazar*, sever, and cut off hell.

Sever and cut off the attacks of hell with your bold words of authority. Command demons to go. Command them, don't ask. Tell them to go. Command healing to come. Command harvest to come. Command revival to come. Command awakening to come. Speak with authority. Use king language.

Prayer

Lord, take us to a higher level as we decree Your Word and bind the works of hell. Let a functioning Kingdom aligned with You, who speaks as You speak, begin to move through this world. Come to us in greater manifestations of Your glory.

6
Obtaining Mode

We decree this is the era of open doors for miracles and the completion of miracles that we have been standing for.

The prophetic words and decrees of faith from long ago are coming together like a battering ram opening doors to a new season. They have prepared us to rise up and define this moment. Strategies of good warfare are providing pathways to victory after victory after victory. We are in a different era; we are not fighting the same battles we used to fight. We are fighting to engage in victories, not just to survive. We are not in survival mode, we are in obtaining mode, and that must become our mindset. It's time to obtain the victories. This era is going to be marked by a Church that is triumphant and moving in victory. The world has never seen anything quite like the New Testament Church that's going to arise.

The prayers, the all-nighters, the tears of intercession, the Lord says, are all coming together now. The identity of the New Testament Church is entering a destiny change to represent Christ and His Kingdom government as intended. We are entering into a supernatural era, the most supernatural era that the Kingdom of God has ever had on the earth. We are pregnant with promises that are to be birthed. We are moving into a miraculous movement moment.

Prophetic words and prophetic dreams are intersecting their moment. The great harvest, outpouring, awakening, and reformation promised have intersected their God-prepared moment. The Ekklesia of King Jesus has come to its moment, which means you and I have come to our moment. We are born-again ones, sons and daughters of God, with the DNA of our Father inside us to subdue and to have dominion on earth, to disciple and bind or loose, to permit or forbid, to represent the mighty Kingdom of Almighty God. His seed is in us, ready to break forth and produce, ready to decree His Word, ways, life, authority, and power.

This is the supernatural, prepared-for season when the Ekklesia finds her voice. We are here to give voice to the will of God on this planet. We are here to voice the governing decrees of our Kingdom to shift a region, a nation, and a world. We are here to give voice to the purpose and the strategies of Almighty God and the mighty Holy Spirit who Jesus declared was our advantage. No matter the odds we always have the advantage.

This era is an era when the glorious Church recognizes her advantage and begins to declare a governing authority. The Ekklesia has been prepared to raise its voice on behalf of a spiritual Kingdom that begins to affect natural kingdoms. We are here to be God's voice to awaken the conscience of a nation and to shift it back to its covenant roots. We can do it, we are prepared to do it, we are authorized to do it, and Holy Spirit and His Angel Armies are here to help us get it done.

PRAYER

Holy Spirit, release Your anointing in me to speak boldly and move swiftly. Fill me with Your Spirit so that everywhere I go, the kingdom of earth will yield to the Kingdom of God.

7

God's Seed

We decree that we are made like our Father and nothing is impossible with God!

Through the parenting seed, character traits, mannerisms, tendencies, and likes or dislikes are passed on to the offspring. Preferences, actions, and hereditary dispositions are inherited through the parents' seed. This is true in our own family, as it is in yours. Neither my daughter, Rachel, nor I can talk without using our hands. We also have very similar temperaments. Our son, Joshua, is very much like his mother. They have similar personalities and leadership skills. It's interesting and fun to notice these things.

Because God's seed is in us, certain tendencies of His will be passed on. This is why believers whose minds are renewed by God's Word can believe that miracles are still possible on earth. Why? Because we're God's seed; we are His children, and He is the Miracle Worker. It is sown into our new nature to have that leaning.

The world does not believe that all things are possible. But Christians whose minds are renewed by God's Word can easily believe such a thing. It's a hereditary trait inside us. We tend to express power. Why? It's in our nature. It was seeded into us at our new birth. We tend to think with authority. We are predisposed that way because God's parenting seed is in us, and He is the highest authority. He has passed that on to us. We tend to believe for dominion, to see ourselves ruling, reigning, and conquering. These are hereditary leanings in the redeemed ones because we're God's seed. His disposition as the ruler of all is planted into us, into our nature, and it's very real.

This is why 1 John 4:4 (AMP) says, *"Little children (believers, dear ones), you are of God and you belong to Him and have [already] overcome them [the agents of the antichrist]; because He who is in you is greater than he (Satan) who is in the world [of sinful mankind]."* God is in us. He has planted His seed into us through His Word. His disposition to always overcome evil is planted into our very nature as part of our spiritual DNA. He has seeded into the nature of His children to never give up, but rather to subdue, conquer, and reign in Jesus' Name.

The tendency of God's kids is to think thoughts filled with hope. It's in the seed passed on to us. We don't need an outside source because we have an inner source. It's a well that springs up inside us. Hope is a genetic marker inside the redeemed, a genetic code in us if we will let it spring up. We are the offspring of the God of hope. That's true for every fruit of the Spirit. The fruit of the Spirit is the nature of God—love, joy, peace, longsuffering, gentleness, goodness, faith, meekness, and temperance (Galatians 5:22-23). We don't need an outside source of joy. Joy is seeded inside us. It's our tendency when we redeem our minds to be joyful, no matter what is thrown our way. Peace is also seeded into us, living inside us. When our mind is renewed, we have peace in the midst of our storms.

PRAYER

God, renew my mind today to see as You see. Give me Your vision. May hope be my lens, always anchoring me to be more aware of the realities of Heaven than the realities of earth.

8
CHILDREN OF GOD

We decree His Word is in our mouth and we will not back down.

Have you ever wondered why you feel so different from the rest of the world? Do you ever think that those around you who are not born again seem like foreigners? It's like they speak a foreign language. Where did they come up with those crazy ideas? But you know they believe the things they say. Do you ever wonder why you think so differently? It's because you have inherited genetic leanings that cause you to think differently. You're God's seed, His child. It is in you to be different. In fact, if you live contrary to God's seed, your conscience is going to bother you because the Holy Spirit in you is going to say, "No, stop it. Don't do that. That's not who you are." You are His child.

Your Father's likes and dislikes have been passed on to you. God's character traits are at work in you, desiring to grow and mature. *You're an heir of God and a joint heir with Christ Jesus* (see Romans 8:17). Renew your mind to it. Transform your thinking by meditating on who God's Word says you really are. Practice Paul's admonition in Romans 12:2 (AMP): *"And do not be conformed to this world [any longer with its superficial values and customs], but be transformed and progressively changed [as you mature spiritually] by the renewing of your mind [focusing on godly values and ethical attitudes], so that you may prove [for yourselves] what the will of God is, that which is good and acceptable and perfect [in His plan and purpose for you]."*

We need to reprogram our minds to think like children of God. To think like one born into a dynasty family of governing authority—the God dynasty. We must think like one living the mandate of God to exercise dominion on earth in His Name, activating real Christian living. Amazingly, God wants to reproduce Himself in you. He wants His image, likeness, and life to grow in you. He wants you to rule and reign with Him. You were born of God to have dominion, not to be dominated by hell, society, culture, or government. Your DNA reads *Overcomer*. Your DNA says *Dominator*. Your DNA declares *Ruler with my Father*. He wants you to be an activated heir, restored in purpose and identity as His offspring to create with words that agree with His words. Like your Father, you, as a child of God, create with words that are seeds.

As His seed on the earth, He wants you to create with "word seed" decrees—create atmospheres for miracles, parameters for society to live in, and an environment that produces life and destroys death. Father God wants His seed in you to release His creative abilities on earth. It's time to recognize that we have God's traits passed on to us. We are heirs with authority delegated to us to be a ruling species of beings. Father's DNA is in us.

PRAYER

Father God, You've placed Your DNA in me. May I partner with that reality, releasing hope, joy, and life through my words and actions wherever I go.

9

Stewarding the Miraculous

We decree our faith is rising and we receive a fresh outpouring of divine healing.

We must see healings and miracles amp up. It's one of the greatest evangelism tools that we have. There is nothing like seeing a blind eye opened, or seeing a cripple healed to open people up to the Gospel. Suddenly, there are people willing to listen.

The coming generation that is constantly on my heart has not seen healings and miracles like I have, and they have to see them. I believe now is the time, and I believe it now has become part of my apostolic assignment. I believe our Ekklesia hubs will now emphasize healings and miracles at new levels as Holy Spirit renews the days of the "Voice of Healing" in even greater ways than the 1950s and '60s. In fact, I'm strong enough in my faith now to prophesy to you that it will happen. It will happen! It is happening! These apostolic Ekklesia hubs are also going to be healing hubs. Dramatic and stunning healings and supernatural miracles have been prophesied to now accelerate. Holy Spirit has planned for them.

Of course, the Ekklesia hubs, and we ourselves, must pray for it. That's our stewardship responsibility. We have to pray and decree for these days to accelerate forward and stand in faith for them because healing is the children's bread. It's God's will to heal. Jesus is our Healer. He healed all manner of sicknesses and diseases. You can go back in New Testament times and see Him do it. He gave His apostles power to go do it. In the book of Acts, they also did it. All things are possible. Holy Spirit is saying, "*Raise your faith now; receive a fresh outpouring of divine healing.*"

Holy Spirit is revealing pieces of His plan and a movement has been launched. God is up to something big, something worldwide. An outpouring that is activating the precedent seen in the New Testament and seen in the book of Acts is now to be contended for and declared to be.

We have moved now into a supernatural era of outpourings of the Holy Spirit that will release healing anointings and activate the gift of healings and workings of miracles described in 1 Corinthians 12 at a new level. Of course, healing is always available. I know that. And we have heard great testimonies, but we need to keep pressing in and believing for them in greater measure.

I am burdened for those who don't know what to do. They feel hopeless. They have not been taught well, or perhaps not at all. They don't even know healing is available. They don't know how to grow their faith. They've been told it's not even for now.

The Healing Movement is a heritage that we have to tap into by teaching it, praying it, and declaring our faith for it to accelerate in Ekklesia hubs everywhere.

Prayer

Holy Spirit, You've moved in great power before, releasing signs, wonders, and miracles that reveal who You are. Do it again. Increase our faith to see the impossible bow its knee to King Jesus! More, Lord!

10

Indisputable Evidence

We decree our King's validation will spring forth in signs, wonders, and miracles.

Jesus spoke to me that we are in the most supernatural era ever. In this miraculous era, King Jesus is stepping up to center stage in amped up, very visible ways. His glory presence, His power, and His Kingdom on earth are becoming manifestly real. As the true Ekklesia steps up to the King's side, led by Holy Spirit, with fiery passion and faithful commitment, it demonstrates that we are indeed heirs and joint heirs with Christ.

Just as Jesus went into cities, villages, and towns, taking center stage healing people of all manner of sicknesses and diseases, we want to see Jesus take center stage again through hundreds of His Kingdom churches and heal all manner of sickness and diseases in all of them at the same time.

We are seeing another part of the Godhead strategy beginning to unfold right in front of us. We are seeing an anointing to cause the Scriptures to come alive in such a way that it changes history. We are seeing the quickening of Christ's healing covenant that is upon His Word describing healings and miracles beginning to rise, and grabbing the attention and soaking the Ekklesias around the world. In this era, the Word of God is being made alive in amazing ways and in some ways that have never been seen before.

The world is about to see at greater levels God's Word confirmed with signs, wonders, miracles, and great healings. It is confirmed as described in Mark 16:20: *"The disciples preached everywhere, the Lord working with them, confirming the Word preached with signs, wonders, miracles, and healings following"* (my paraphrase).

The word *Lord* there is the Greek word *kurios* (Strong's G2962) and it means "the Supreme Commander or the Supreme One." It also means "Master with supreme authority" and it means "the One who has all authority or supreme authority." One definition of *kurios* that I really like—the word *Lord* means "the Owner." The Owner of the earth worked with them.

Today, the Owner of the earth is stepping to center stage to work with us just as He did with the early disciples.

> And the disciples went everywhere preaching, the Master working right with them, validating the Message with indisputable evidence (Mark 16:20 MSG).

Evidence they couldn't dispute. He worked with them confirming indisputable evidence.

King Jesus is stepping to center stage to work through His Ekklesias, confirming the message they are preaching with signs, wonders, miracles, and healings. Think about this and its meaning. The Lord Himself—Jesus—in His omnipresent self, working with us to confirm His Word in all Ekklesias with validating evidence. Validation is coming to Scriptures that for years we have declared and stood for.

The word *sign* is the Greek word *semeion* (Strong's G4592), and it means "miracles that indicate a connection to grace and power from Heaven, activated by Holy Spirit." We are connecting to a grace and power that Heaven is giving to indisputably validate the message that we are preaching.

This is part of the history-changing era that we have been told we are already in: Holy Spirit's most supernatural era. The King takes center stage with His Bride, His Church, by His side, and what His Bride declares, He will now personally oversee as the King overseeing His plan.

Prayer

God of Glory, may Your ways and Your works be seen on the earth once again, validating the preaching of the Gospel and drawing all people to Yourself. Anoint us for this hour, this miraculous era.

11

GROWING A MIRACLE

We decree that we will believe and keep on believing what God says.

This is a season of open doors for miracles. The people of God in this new era are going to grow miracles to fullness. This is a scriptural view that isn't explained the way it should be; and because of it, people suffer hope deferred. Some people lose their faith and confidence where miracles are concerned. There are times when miracles must be grown by faith. It happens individually and it happens corporately. Some miracles take time to grow to fullness.

God can sovereignly do miracles, and He sometimes does that. He can do miracles whenever He wants, but because of a fallen planet He has recused Himself from doing that very often. I'm not talking about sovereign miracles; I'm talking about partnering with God to see miracles happen by faith.

One of the greatest examples of growing a miracle is seen in Mary, Joseph, and Jesus. Christ's birth certainly is a miracle, but we must admit that He was not ready to become our sacrifice for sin until many years after His birth. The miracle of who He was grew to reveal the greatest miracle ever. He was a miracle who had to grow to completion. We also see that there was miracle after miracle after miracle within the growing of the greatest Miracle ever. This is what is accelerating in our time now.

Growing, by definition, requires the passage of time, which is something that we don't usually equate with miracles. Let's face it, we want our miracle now. We want instant, zapped, and done right now. If there is the passage of time between a miracle's conception and its completion, often doubt creeps in and unbelief seeks a place to pollute our thinking that nothing is happening and nothing is going to happen. If not resisted, this aborts the miracle.

Because of the passage of time, millions cast away their confidence and give up on receiving a miracle. Many today are skeptics where miracles are concerned because of hope deferred, circumstances, feelings, and life on a fallen planet. This is often promoted by a nominal church that openly states, "Miracles are not for today."

Because of life on a fallen planet, our faith constantly finds obstacles that it has to overcome. It finds disease, unfair attacks, situations, and circumstances that have to be overcome. Forget fairness; lucifer and his kingdom are never going to be fair. Ever. It's never going to happen. If you focus on the fairness of something, your emotions are going to control you. Forget it and focus your faith on what God says. Believe and keep on believing what God says. You believe until you receive.

Prayer

Lord Jesus, I pray for an upgrade of faith today. Increase my faith to believe You and Your Word! My faith is rising and I will believe it until I receive it!

12

THE GOOD FIGHT OF FAITH

We declare that we will believe and not grow faint.

In Scripture, the angel Gabriel comes to Mary and he tells her that she is now going to bear the Son of God. He tells her the Messiah is going to be supernaturally placed in her womb. She is personally visited by one of the most powerful angels that God ever created. But after that visit there was nothing. It's not like Gabriel came every year and then reinforced that. Elizabeth did confirm it when Jesus was in Mary's womb, and the wise men confirmed it when He was two years old, but there were no other words of promise that came to her that we know of. None. From then on she simply had to walk it out by faith. That is truly amazing when you think about it for this young lady. From then on she simply had to keep growing the miracle. No other words came the next year. No other promises came 10 years later or 20 years later or 25 years later. None. She just kept believing that one word.

We see in this something very important that must be understood where miracles are concerned. Some delays are demonic and need to be bound in Christ's Name. Some miracles are delayed by flesh or other adversity and they also need to be bound. Still other miracles are delayed because of the corporate sins of a nation and must be overcome. But some delays are simply the passage of time and the miracle has to grow to completion. The Bible reveals that some delay is a gestation period to grow the miracle and to get everything or everyone in its proper place.

This doesn't mean God's not working and nothing is happening. It doesn't mean God's not preparing things and there will be no miracle. Remember, the miracle of God was working just as much when Jesus was five years old as when He was born or 30. The miracle was working the entire time and it never stopped. It's just that most of the time it could not be seen progressing.

But we know, according to God's Word, the miracle had not stopped. It was still growing. Preparation for its completion was still moving forward. It was just happening in ways that Mary and Joseph couldn't see. Some miracles are instant, but some are going to grow or be grown in the atmosphere of faith over time. In fact, a whole lot of them are. We need to discern the difference, understanding both are miracles and both are supernatural. Oftentimes, the greatest miracles are those that are completed after extended times of standing and believing and fighting, as Paul said, "The good fight of faith."

Mary and Joseph's testimony teaches us if the miracle isn't completed instantly, then it's in the process of being completed. Keep on believing. Keep learning—perhaps there's a key that needs to be revealed to you. Keep listening—perhaps there's some instructions that you need to be following. Keep following Holy Spirit—perhaps He needs to lead you to the right place, person, or situation. A counselor, an advisor, a physician, a procedure, a way you don't know. A way you may never have heard of. Keep following and saying what God says. We are never told Mary or Joseph ever abandoned what God promised them. They never gave up on it. When doubt crept in, which happens to us all, they resisted it and they kept believing what God said.

Prayer

Holy Spirit, activate in my memory today words You have spoken that I need to declare. I refocus my faith on Your nature—You never lie. You are always good, and I know You are always working. I will keep following and saying what You say!

13

THE ASSIGNMENT OF HIS WORD

We decree angels are organizing around the prayers of God's people, helping to bring them to pass.

> "I don't think the way you think. The way you work isn't the way I work." God's Decree. "For as the sky soars high above earth, so the way I work surpasses the way you work, and the way I think is beyond the way you think. Just as rain and snow descend from the skies and don't go back until they've watered the earth, doing their work of making things grow and blossom, producing seed for farmers and food for the hungry, so will the words that come out of my mouth not come back empty-handed. They'll do the work I sent them to do, they'll complete the assignment I gave them" (Isaiah 55:8-11 MSG).

Notice that God's prophetic words, dreams, and visions to us have assignments that He has breathed on, and they are empowered to do what He says when His people stand in faith for them. Prophetic words are connecting now to their moment, corporately and individually. It is true for your life, your family, your business, vocation, and ministry; it is across the board. God's promises will connect to their moment.

In Daniel 9, we see this principle of prophetic words intersecting with their moment as prophetic prayers, strategies, and instructions concerning a new era play out in an extremely dramatic way. It's a prayer of Daniel that is instructive as well as fascinating. This is a prayer that absolutely changed history by changing a nation. It activated prophetic promises and caused Heaven to respond, and it caused the release of angel princes and their armies from Heaven. It is a prayer that bound a demon prince and overthrew his reign over an entire region.

We must understand that the Bible is not only a history of what has happened but is also instructive for today. We are in Holy Spirit times, just like Daniel or any of the prophets or apostles. They were not a different class of people than we are. They were in a spiritual realm that is available to us, as well. They were God's people, just as we are. Respect them, absolutely, but do not deify them. As born-again believers, we too are in Holy Spirit times of God-appointed, powerful angelic assistance. We can, and we should, experience supernatural Kingdom of God activity. Actually, because of a new covenant and the baptism of the Holy Spirit, we should experience it even more so.

Remember, Daniel was praying for wisdom concerning his nation and the future. God heard his prayer the first day he started praying and sent the angel, Gabriel, with the answer to that prayer. Gabriel said, "I'm here to help you understand the strategy that the King has for your future. There is a future and it is good. I'm here to assist and answer your prayers" (see Daniel 9:22-23). Clearly, God assigns angels to answer prayers. They organize around the prayers of God's people, helping to bring them to pass.

Prayer

Lord Jesus, thank You for the angels who beckon to Your Word. Thank You that the angelic is now being dispatched to bring Your words and promises into alignment for this day and this hour. Ready us, Lord, for what You are about to do.

14

From Conception to Completion

We declare You are taking us into a new season spawning miracle after miracle after miracle!

Prophetic words must be taken very seriously. At The Oasis, we reread them, pray them, and decree them over and over. There are very few times when we meet for prayer that I don't read a prophetic word that we are to pray and decree, reemphasizing the importance of the prophetic words of God. I remember as a child, growing up in church, when a prophetic word was given and we didn't remember what was said by the next week. Nobody paid any attention. It was just something that made us feel good. Many received personal prophetic words and they forget all about them a short time later. Nothing came to fruition because it wasn't grown to completion. We have to take them seriously.

God's Word doesn't return void if somebody believes it. Twenty years ago I remember I was sitting at the end of the church parking lot when I said, "What You said I will believe, and I will never back down from it." I have fought a lot of wars over that but I still believe today what God said.

Somebody has to stand for God's prophetic word until we experience completion of that word. Someone has to act on them; they don't sovereignly happen. We have to understand if God said it He wants us to live in it and be resourced by it.

When the people of God left Egyptian bondage under the great leader Moses, they were pursuing a promise, a dream, a miracle over 400 years old. The journey to that actual promise was 40 years. Four decades. We see over time as they pursued that ultimate dream, the Promised Land, miracle after miracle after miracle was spawned. The Red Sea opened. Manna fell on the ground and fed over a million people every day. Quails were flown in to feed them all. An entire river flowed from a granite mountainside to quench their thirst. Plagues of disease were stopped and thousands were healed. These were genuine miracles experienced on their way to the gigantic miracle that had been promised years before.

One of the things that amazes me, as I have studied and thought about this great Exodus, is how most of that generation of people abandoned God's promise and died in the wilderness. They never obtained the promise because of unbelief. These were people who had experienced the miracles I just listed and many more. They saw them with their own eyes. It wasn't a report that somebody gave to them about a miracle they saw; they had lived it themselves. Yet, because of the passage of time, because it wasn't instant, they gave up. I have said to the Lord many times, "I don't want to die in the wilderness with the murmurers and complainers. I want to be part of Joshua and Caleb's remnant that crossed over and possessed their promise." I want to finish the journey from conception to completion.

Thankfully, we have a choice. We can believe and keep on believing, stand and can keep on standing until one day we receive and keep on receiving.

God has given us prophetic words and promises. He has given us these words so that we could live in them, not just know them. He has called us to steward them, to grow them with our faith, to believe them from the time we receive them until the time they are completed. To believe them all and everything He said and not back off. To believe them all from conception to completion.

PRAYER

Lord, I ask for a persistent faith that presses through and keeps on believing. May we be those like Joshua and Caleb who saw the promise of the Promised Land. Increase our faith. Anchor our trust. Our sights are set on You.

15

Revival Wells Uncapped

We decree bend us, bend us, bend us.

Hear what Holy Spirit is saying: "*It's time for old healing wells and revival wells to be uncapped. Awakening angels are connecting us to Holy Spirit strategies with past streams of revival and past anointings that are now activating in our times.*" New streams for our times are flowing and new anointings are synergizing together. It is time to see all of this; it's time for our future to change. A move of God is beginning that cannot be stopped.

Several years ago, Carol and I drove up to Canada to minister at a conference. We arrived late in the afternoon and only had a little bit of time to freshen up at the hotel before being picked up to go to the meeting place. I was ready to go and waiting for Carol and only had enough time to ask, "Holy Spirit, why am I here? What are You saying?" Immediately the Lord spoke these words to me: "*The revival in Canada will be like the Welsh Revival led by Evan Roberts.*" I wrote those words down, someone picked us up, and off we went to the meeting.

When we arrived, we stepped through the back door of an old hockey arena that held around 500 people. We were led through the door, past the platform and pulpit, to seats in the front row. When we walked in, I saw that the leader of the meeting had placed an old wooden chair near the pulpit, which I thought was a little unusual, but I didn't mention it. As I met with the leader prior to starting the meeting, she said to me, "Do you see that chair? That's Evan Roberts' chair from the Welsh Revival." I nearly fell over because of what Holy Spirit had spoken to me back in the hotel. I reached for my Bible and handed her the paper that had the words I had written just an hour earlier: "The revival in Canada will be like the Welsh Revival led by Evan Roberts."

I had no idea, had never been in that arena before, and I certainly didn't know they were going to have that chair there. But Holy Spirit did, and He knew it would start speaking to us. Holy Spirit is saying to us, "Remember the Welsh Revival. Pick up the mantle of the Welsh Revival." This prophetic understanding is not just for Canada but also for the United States. Holy Spirit has repeatedly spoken to me that the revival in America will be like the Welsh Revival.

Evan Roberts was a young man who worked in the coal mines; he was also a blacksmith. Today, we would define him as a millennial. Roberts spent hours praying and reading his Bible, often all night long. He was the youth pastor at his church and also taught Sunday school. At the age of 26, after praying and seeking the Lord for days, he felt led to go to a missions conference led by evangelist Seth Joshua. At the end of the meeting, the evangelist prayed a prayer and one particular line was, "Lord, bend us," which was a phrase used in those times for holiness. It's not really used in that way today. In other words, "Bend us to follow You, Lord. Make our hearts pliable. Soften us, Lord. Bend us into who we need to be. Bend my life so it is usable, Lord. Shape us." The Ekklesia needs to pray the same today.

PRAYER

Lord Jesus, as You did in Wales, do right here. Bend us to follow You, Lord. Bend my life. Your Kingdom come right here, right now.

16

THE EFFECTS OF REVIVAL

We decree Heaven's time clock is setting our heart in rhythm with God's heart.

As the Welsh Revival began, Seth Joshua prayed a simple prayer with cataclysmic effect: "Bend us, Lord." Suddenly, people in the congregation began to spontaneously pray out loud. Evan Roberts writes of that moment:

> When others prayed I felt a living force come into my bosom. It held my breath, and my legs shivered. ...The living force grew and grew, and I was almost bursting. ...I cried, "Bend me! Bend me! Bend us!" What bent me was God commending His Love... and I wept. Henceforth the salvation of souls became the burden of my heart. From that time I was on fire with a desire to go through all Wales.[1]

And the young man did just that. Conservative estimates are that over 150,000 gave their hearts to Christ during this time. Bars closed and crime was practically nonexistent. The police actually said they had little to do besides managing the crowds who were going to a

1 "O Lord, Bend Us," Blaenannerch Calvinistic Methodist Chapel—1904-1905 Welsh Revival, *Walesawakening.org;* https://walesawakening.org/revivalhistory/The-Bending-at-Blaenannerch.pdf; accessed July 17, 2025.

revival or church meeting. The people were so joyful, and they sang so much that the revival simply became known as the "Singing Revival."

Thousands of coal miners were saved, many of whom were hard-core sinners. These coal miners now loved to sing while they worked. It was said the mules that carted off the coal had to be retrained because they had been trained by these hard miners to follow the command of curse words; they didn't understand kind words.

The coal mine had large air shafts running hundreds of feet down into the earth all over the Welsh hillsides. People would bring chairs and sit around those air shafts, listening for hours to the reverberating songs and hymns echoing up from the bowels of the earth, from men who were now saved. The songs would travel down the line as various men joined in, singing for so long that all around the hillside you could hear the songs coming up from the earth. No one sings quite like the Welsh; theirs is an accent that gets into your soul. It is so hard to imagine this, but the countryside literally echoed with praise and worship wafting up from the ground. All of Wales was changed, and then the nations around them began to change.

Holy Spirit has released awakening angels now to connect us to the anointings of previous revivals. They are also connecting us to the great awakening that is planned for our times. They are connecting us to prophetic words, visions, and dreams. There are no angel graveyards. The angels from Wales didn't die. They have assisted outpouring after outpouring. We are told in the Scriptures that the angels gain knowledge and understanding. The angels that assisted Holy Spirit in Acts 2 are some of the same angels that are assisting us to this day. They assist the saints in helping minister a fresh move of God upon this earth. It just makes spiritual sense. They are activated and are here to assist us, only they are more experienced now than they ever were before. The Third Great Awakening has begun.

PRAYER

Holy Spirit, thank You for the angelic assistance You have given us to connect us to revivals of the past. Lord, do even today greater works than what You did then! Show us Your glory! May our lands be changed because of Your glorious presence.

17

The Dawning of a New Era

We decree the Ekklesia will rise and rule as intended.

As I was praying and preparing for service one Sunday, I began to feel a prophetic anointing stirring inside me. I continued praying in the Spirit for another 20 minutes or so when Holy Spirit began showing me a vision. Ever since I was a small child, God has shown me visions and then talked to me about their meaning. It's the foremost way in which He speaks to me.

In this vision, I saw a huge funnel, like the type that's used to pour oil into a car's engine, with a big bowl at one end and a stem at the other end. The bowl of the funnel was actually like a television screen, and I began to see various scenes scrolling around the sides of it. There were scenes, one after another, of events down through the ages, including the book of Acts, church history and events, great revivals and prayer meetings, revivalists and evangelists, and other great movements of history. It was as if I was watching a movie. After a while, the scenes began to circle further down into the funnel bowl and were being squeezed into the narrow stem at the bottom, running out into our times.

Not wanting to surmise the meaning, I asked, "Holy Spirit, what are You showing me?" He answered, "I'm pouring the anointings and the streams of Christ's Kingdom throughout the ages into the new era we've prepared for the glorious Ekklesia." I then asked, "What am I to do with this?" He stated, "You are to declare that it is now connected to its moment. The synergy and convergence of the ages have begun. The anointings and outpourings have begun. The activation of prophetic words has begun. Pray it, decree it, prophesy it, guard it. Steward its activation into your times."

His words then became like a prophecy: "For you have entered a fullness of time and are entering the second apostolic age, an era of signs, wonders and miracles." This was the second time Holy Spirit talked to me about the second apostolic age. "It is the era," said the Lord, "when the Ekklesia sits on the throne of their regions and influences the natural realms of earth through the spiritual Kingdom. Watch the Ekklesia rise, for it shall surely rise. It is purposed. It shall be so. It will rise and it will rule as intended, for it has now connected to its moment. Watch the change and the changes. Align with Heaven and you will see it on earth. Align with Heaven and activate the rapid change. Speak your agreement. Speak to the fog. Command it to lift and you will see the new era."

PRAYER

Lord, let Your surge begin on earth. Let a functioning Kingdom aligned with You begin to move through this world. Come to us in greater manifestations of Your glory.

18

DAYS OF GREAT POWER

We declare the Ekklesia is now partnering with Holy Spirit and rising to bring the Kingdom of Heaven to earth.

We have moved into days of power being amped up to much higher levels within the Ekklesia. Prophetic dreams, visions, prophecies, and Scriptures we have been decreeing are now accelerating. Holy Spirit has been prophesying into our times, which is designed to give us great hope, raise our faith, and activate delegated authority at levels we've never operated in before.

Holy Spirit is releasing Godhead plans and strategies, whereby the supernatural is merging into the natural or the earth realm. Those who have said the gifts of Holy Spirit are not for today will be proven wrong. Those who say the days of miracles are over will be proven wrong by the number of miracles that are going to be seen. World-shaking miracles are coming into the earth realm. The power of the Living God has not diminished, and His greatest move on the planet is now unfolding.

The world and its cocky arrogance rising to try to stop it will fail. Demon power won't stop it. Fools in government, media, and big tech won't stop it. Baal's antichrist doctrines and laws will not stop it. Only a fool would dare say that God can no longer do something. He can do whatever He wants to do.

When God decides to move, He has always found a willing remnant. He anoints that remnant, led by the Holy Spirit, to accomplish a purpose or a plan that He has in mind. He has already done that in this era. The remnant has been anointed and taught.

Holy Spirit is an all-powerful member of the Godhead. He is who we're partnering with. The depth of His abilities cannot even be measured. His wisdom and skills are constantly seen in His omnipresent, all-knowing, all-powerful being. The One Jesus described as His other self to His disciples has been sent to be with us and in us. And He is here to endue us with power from Heaven.

Holy Spirit was sent to baptize us in the enablement of Heaven. He is here to come alongside us to implement the authority of King Jesus that has been delegated to us in His Name. Our mission is not helpless. Our assignment is not hopeless. We have a divine member of the Godhead who is with us at all times. He is not here in a diminished capacity. Nothing is too hard for Him. The supernatural is His natural; it's His normal. The complexities of our world do not overwhelm Him.

In this season, we have been assured that the Godhead has said once again, "It's time. Implement the plan." Holy Spirit is moving in supernatural ways to get that done.

We must understand that we, the Ekklesia today, are to move in supernatural power and ways. It is part of His plan. The Ekklesia is supposed to flow in the supernatural abilities of Holy Spirit. That's what we are being called to at this moment.

PRAYER

Lord Jesus, we ask that You stretch our faith now to prepare us for what You are about to pour out in our midst! Come, Holy Spirit in Your power and might!

19

Kingdom Revival

We decree the world will see and know the love of our Father, the love of our King, setting captives free and healing the sick.

Kingdom revivals involve notable miracles. The Scripture behind this is found in Acts 3 and 4, shortly after the outpouring of Holy Spirit in Acts 2. Peter and John were going to the temple for the 3 o'clock prayer meeting. On their way, they had to pass through the temple gate that is called the Gate Beautiful, where a lame man sat begging for money. This man was 40 years old and had been crippled from birth.

Hundreds of thousands of people had walked by this man as he lay by the gate. Jesus Himself had passed by this man many times. But on this day, Holy Spirit was pressing and emphasizing miracles to the Jerusalem Ekklesia.

Peter and John had heard what Holy Spirit had been pressing and saying. They also knew firsthand the miraculous healing power of Jesus. They could personally tell hundreds of testimonies of healings that they had witnessed. They were with Jesus when He had healed cripples. They were standing right beside Him when blind eyes were opened.

As they approached the gate called Beautiful, Holy Spirit filled them with a surge of power and great boldness. Peter fastened his eyes on the lame beggar and said, "Look up here at us." And when he did, expecting to receive alms or a donation, Peter said, "I'm not giving you silver, and I'm not giving you gold. I've got something for you that money cannot buy. In the Name of Jesus Christ of Nazareth, rise up and walk." Then he grabbed his hands and pulled this man to his feet. Immediately his feet and ankle bones received strength, and this man leaped and began to run, glorifying God through the temple.

Muscles, bones, and an ankle that had never been used instantly received strength. And beyond that, this man, who for 40 years had never walked, had a miracle take place in his brain. Signals that weren't good before in this man's brain suddenly became good; balance was supernaturally provided. People were astounded as they watched this lame man they had passed by for years, jumping and running throughout the temple. Who wouldn't be astounded?

Well, amazingly, the religious leaders, the priests, and the Pharisees didn't like it. Can you imagine that? They felt it would diminish their importance or influence, so they had Peter and John arrested for doing this. The next day, Peter and John were brought before the council and asked by whose authority did they do this for this man. Peter and John answered, "Jesus, the resurrected Lord, that you guys crucified. We did it in His Name." Through faith in His Name, this man has been made whole.

Acts 4:15-16 (NKJV) says, *"But when they had commanded them to go aside out of the council, they conferred among themselves, saying, 'What shall we do to these men? For, indeed, that a notable miracle has been done through them is evident to all who dwell in Jerusalem, and we cannot deny it.'"*

In other words, "It's too obvious. We can't deny this. We can't bury it." And they had to let them go.

Now, in another apostolic age, on the edge of another Kingdom revival and to other Ekklesias, Holy Spirit is saying again to press into the miraculous and healing realm, to press into the supernatural and believe for notable miracles to now leap forward in the Name of Jesus.

PRAYER

Holy Spirit, baptize me again with Your presence today. Open my eyes to see the miraculous. Give me the faith to follow You wherever You lead, seeing Heaven break through in every part of my life. Help me to press in and not lose focus.

20

ONLY GOD

We decree all of the words, visions, dreams, and prophecies will accomplish their assignment! Notable miracles are in season.

Holy Spirit is saying you are now moving into days when notable miracles are accelerating forward through Kingdom Ekklesias. They are flowing into towns, cities, regions, states, nations, and religions. They will be forced to admit God did that.

> What should we do with these men? Everyone in Jerusalem can clearly see that they've performed a notable sign and wonder—we can't deny that (Acts 4:16 TPT).

The word *notable* is the Greek word *gnóstos* (Strong's G1110) and it means "known." It is also the word for "great, knowable, perceive, recognizable, capable of being known." In other words, they are miracles that anyone can perceive is a miracle. *Gnostos* refers to a very clear visible and a great miracle.

Gnostos is derived from *gnoston*, and it means that which is known to be only from God. It means a known manifestation of God's power beyond the natural realm. It's supernatural. *Gnoston* references "only God" power. Only God can do that. Only God possibilities. Only God manifestations. Only God workings. Only God accomplishments. Only God actions. Only God deeds.

In other words, notable miracles are miracles only God can do and everybody knows it. It's God-action on earth that can't be denied. It's God's power manifesting through His apostles and His heirs. It is a sign that says, "God did that," and only He could. Notable signs are seeing paralyzed people running and jumping after 40 years: you can't deny it.

> "I want you to believe Me for the supernatural power of the Living God to come into your churches and lives. Believe Me for God possibilities. Believe for God-action to start being released around you. Believe for God manifestations and deeds. Believe for God accomplishments to flow through your life."

We must believe for notable miracles that get the attention of the world. Believe for notable miracles that prodigals can witness. Believe for signs and wonders that unbelievers can see. It will get their attention and they will know that Jesus is Lord.

The Lord has said we are stepping into His most supernatural era. Part of every era is signs, wonders, miracles, and healings, and *notable healings* or *notable miracles*. It is a precedent in all eras, and we must grow our faith now, daring to ask for the double portion. We are not going to change history without the supernatural.

Raise your faith level. Believe the same works, the same healing power, the same miracles Jesus did, we shall do, also. Not by our power, but by the same Spirit, Holy Spirit, who raised Christ from the dead.

It is now time to follow the lead of Holy Spirit into supernatural times, supernatural manifestations of signs and wonders. It's time to receive His anointings for signs, wonders, miracles, healings, and notable miracles.

Prayer

Holy Spirit, I will follow Your lead! Father God, come in power and pour out signs, wonders, and miracles the world has never seen before!

21

THE SHAKING HAS BEGUN

We decree that the arrows of the Lord's deliverance will hit the mark!

I believe God wants to give breakthrough to our nation. It's connecting to its moment, it's time. He is saying, "*Church, you need to pray. Just as the prophet Elijah birthed the rain in prayer, you must birth this in prayer. Decree the breakthrough that I have promised you.*"

Something very big is up, and a shift in our nation can now occur. Though we may experience times of crises, we see throughout the Word of God, and throughout history, those are the times when breakthroughs begin to manifest. The true Ekklesia will rise up—not backing off—and what God says and has said will come to pass.

I recall a portion of a prophetic word I had given at one of our Prophetic Summits concerning a remnant that was willing to press in and pray for a Third Great Awakening:

> "Great revival fire will burn throughout the world as My greatest awakening begins to move. Regions and entire nations will become activated in My increasing glory. My shaking will come.
>
> "Walls, strongholds, obstacles of hell's fortification are being shaken down, even as you are being shaken free.

"My shakings will open ancient wells of revival. I will shake open the capped wells of evangelism. I will shake open the ancient wells of healings, miracles, and mighty deliverance. I will shake down the barricades to new roads.

"The Lord of Hosts decrees new roads, new inroads, new mantles, new vision, and new harvest! Behold, I do new things and you shall know it and see it springing forth.

"Because your cries have come up before Me and because your worship has pursued My presence, the head of the Church declares over His triumphant remnant: you will now begin reality church.

"The Lord says I am removing the arrows shot in My ministers of righteousness. Arrows of betrayal, arrows from Jezebel, arrows from Absalom, arrows of deceit and gossip born in lying spirits, arrows by those bound by religious demons. I am removing arrows. You will be free. You will be healed. You will be restored and on fire with My presence.

"For I have said, I will make My ministers a flame of fire. It is ordained, your place of pain will become the place you reign. Rise and rule with Me. I am now coming to My remnant as Lord Sabaoth, the Lord of Angel Armies, and for those who align with My purpose, I will now align My hosts to assist.

"Battle lines are drawn. Strategies are in place. Preparations have been made. I will now gather My Angel Armies with My Ekklesia armies in a unified coalition. The coalition of My willing—those who run to battle, not from it.

"My earth and My Heaven army will challenge thrones of iniquity, thrones of idolatry, thrones of rebellion, thrones of witchcraft, humanism, and antichrist demons. Entire divisions of angels are dispatched and await the decree of My words through My heirs."

The shaking has begun. Revival wells are shaking open. Harvests are being shaken free. Signs, wonders, and miracles are shaking free. Breakthroughs are breaking out. A divine shake-up is happening to shake us free.

PRAYER

King Jesus, You are Lord and there is no other. May revival spring up all around the globe, shifting governments and leadership structures until the kingdom of earth looks like the Kingdom of Heaven.

22

For Such a Time as This

We declare a reversal of the prescription of hell for this nation.

As the King's heirs on earth, we have been restored to use authority language. We have been restored to speak with royal dominion. We have been restored to speak royal edicts for our Kingdom. We have received authority in Jesus' Name to stop evil prescriptions and laws and to decree God's prescriptions as His kids. We are here to decree God's statutes, laws, ways, and will. We are here to declare God's prescription for our lives, over our assignments, and for our nation. As Christ's joint heirs, we are here to reign in this life using authority language (see Romans 8:17).

There can be no confusion or ambiguity. Your words must be decisive. Kings who succeed are not negative. Without question, God's Word states clearly that born-again believers' decrees are very, very powerful if they don't make them negative. There is power to change in our decrees. There is power to reverse legislation in our decrees. There is power to reverse evil laws in our decrees, as long as we don't make them negative. The King's anointing—which, of course, is Christ's anointing—to rule and reign in this life does not flow through me if I am negative. Negativity stifles the flow of anointing through you, and God will not be able to do what He wants to do for you. God wants to make you rule and reign, but you can't do that in negativity.

Authority language was given to Mordecai and Esther to decree a stop to evil laws, to stop an attack against God's people. Kingly language to change a nation was given to them. I see a very strong parallel that pictures the calling of God to His people and to His church right now. In my nation, evil laws are already on the books. Abortion is already a law. Gay marriage is already a law. Even though God says it's an abomination, our legislators have already put it into the law of the land.

It's time for the Church to rise up, to do and say what God says, speaking with authority, pronouncing a different prescription. We must rise up in faith and trust our Almighty Great God, ruling in the midst of our enemies. The insanity has to stop, and it can only be stopped by a real Church, not a pretend one.

My prayer is the apostles' prayer in Acts 4:29 (KJV), "*Lord, behold their threatenings: and grant unto thy servants, that with all boldness they may speak thy word.*" It is crucial that the Church hear the challenges in our midst and, like Esther, intercede. She prayed and made an appeal. Like Esther and Mordecai, we too must rise up for such a time as this.

Prayer

Almighty God, let Your Church awaken. Awaken Your people by the millions to make a stand right now to raise their voice and decree their authority, their faith, and their confidence in You.

23
THE TIME TO TRIUMPH

We decree notable deliverance is now in season and it is breaking out all around the world and in our lives.

In the Modern English Version, the apostle Paul says in 2 Corinthians 2:14, *"Thanks be to God who always causes us to triumph in Christ...."* In this supernatural era when King Jesus takes center stage and His Ekklesia, His remnant, believers step to His side, Holy Spirit is pouring out the breaker anointing of King Jesus to help us triumph in very difficult and dark times. This is true in our personal lives as well as throughout the nations. He is causing us to triumph in evil times.

This is an era when God's people are going to experience great victories, great deliverance. God's words of miraculous power to break oppression of all types—spirit, soul, and body—are being released. His promises are now connecting to their moment, and it is going to change things for thousands and thousands of people.

God is validating His promises with signs, wonders, miracles, and healings. Part of the wonder of this moment—part of the miraculous power of God seen in this era—is going to be the anointing on sons and daughters to win great battles and victories.

In fact, in the definition of the word *triumph* itself is the picture of a celebratory parade of victory, like hosanna—a palm victory, where they waved the palm branches because it symbolized great victory. It is a time of triumph.

Part of a recent prophetic word released to us said, *"The Lord of Hosts decrees the loosing of My people from yokes of bondage."*

A yoke, of course, is the wooden beam that went across the neck of oxen, and leather straps then tied that yoke around the neck of the oxen and were attached to a plow or possibly a wagon. In other words, a yoke ties you to what you are plowing. You're plowing, or dragging, a great weight behind you, a weight that is sapping your strength. It's slowing you down, and it's wearing you out.

> "The Lord of Host decrees the loosing of My people from yokes of bondage. I will break the back of the oppressors. I will loose miracles among you. Believe Me for miracles. Believe Me for signs and wonders. Believe Me for healings of all manner of sickness and disease. Believe Me for long-awaited miracles. Believe me for notable miracles and healings. And believe me for notable deliverance."

As I reread that word, the last line jumped out at me: *"Believe me for notable deliverance."* God's Word describes times when notable deliverance is seen and God acts on His promises. When God's words of promise come to their moment, He acts with great power, validating it and bringing it to pass. We are in that moment right now.

We have entered a fight that we have never entered into before, but understand from Alpha's position to the ending position, there is going to be triumph. Something has to be overcome. We are called overcomers, meaning ones who, with God's help, overcome.

We are the ones who come over. We are called conquerors but you cannot be a conqueror unless you conquer something. Holy Spirit says, *"I'm leading you into times when I'm pouring out anointing to conquer."* It is going to require faith and tenacity. It's going to require courage on our part, but fresh anointing is producing supernatural deliverance.

Prayer

Lord, I ask for Your breakthrough to come and come quickly. May Your triumph be great and be put on display so that the world will know You are the rightful King.

24

He Who Holds My Hand

We decree You are with us at all times; You never leave or forsake us.

We are moving into times when King Jesus personally goes before us to fight battles with us, to bring us victory, and to break us through. That is this season. He's coming to center stage with His people to break them through. This theme occurs throughout the Word of God. If you trust Him, He will break you through. If you trust Him, He will cause you to triumph. He will personally lead you to great victories. Jesus said to His disciples, *"Be sure of this, I am with you at all times. Don't forget that. I am with you always."* Hear those words as a *rhema* word, as a word being breathed by the Godhead into our times, to us right now. These words are being freshly quickened into this moment. I AM is personally rising up to go before you and bring you great victory and great deliverance.

The Lord declares His prophetic word through the prophet Isaiah:

> Don't panic. I'm with you. There's no need to fear for I'm your God. I'll give you strength. I'll help you. I'll hold you steady, keep a firm grip on you. Count on it: Everyone who had it in for you will end up out in the cold—real losers. Those who worked against you will end up empty-handed—nothing to show for their lives. When you go out looking for your old adversaries

> you won't find them—not a trace of your old enemies, not even a memory. That's right. Because I, your God, have a firm grip on you and I'm not letting go. I'm telling you, "Don't panic. I'm right here to help you" (Isaiah 41:10-13 MSG).

Picture that image: I'll hold your hand. I will not fail you. I will not let you go. I'll hold on.

When I was a small boy, my mom used to sing a song about this. My dad was an evangelist. Back then we were involved in revivals every week somewhere, or sometimes two-week revivals, and then we moved on to the next one. Once or twice during those revivals, my mom would sing during the worship, "*I don't know about tomorrow, I just live from day to day. I don't borrow from its sunshine, for its skies may turn to gray. I don't worry over the future, for I know what Jesus said. And today I'll walk beside Him, for He knows what is ahead.*"

He's Alpha and Omega, and I know who holds my hand.

> "I know, don't panic, I'm right here. Don't panic, I've got a firm grip. I won't drop you. I'll hold your hand. I'm going to hold you steady during the tough times. I'm going to hold you steady when life becomes difficult. I'm going to hold you steady when the storm comes. Trust Me, I'll be there when you go into war. I'll go with you into battle, trust Me. Put your faith and confidence in Me. Trust what I say. Trust My words of promise. Trust and act in faith, not fear. I will strengthen you, I will help you. Count on it; depend on it."

Prayer

Father, when I am weary, please give me Your strength. Give me eyes to see that You are leading me, making a way where there seems to be no way and bringing the victory. You are Alpha and Omega. My journey is safe with You.

25
Count On It

We decree You are the God of wonders and the God of turnaround. Our trust is in You and You alone.

I'm so thankful that God has held my hand time after time after time through some very difficult situations. I can testify, you can count on Him. He's been there when it looked impossible. He's been there through the good, the bad, and the ugly. You can count on Him. How many times have I felt His presence flood my soul, reassuring me He's with me? Every time.

Sometimes part of the miracle testimony, part of the wonder for me has been—I made it! How in the world did it happen? I made it. He was there every time. He helped me. He personally guided me through. He was there from the beginning to the end. Alpha and Omega. He helped me overcome it.

There are many times Carol and I and our family can testify, if you just keep holding His hand, His delivering promise will be made real to you. It may take awhile, but it will. So many times over the years I made it by holding His hand, and He came through.

"Count on it," He said. And I'm emphasizing it, *count on it.* He's coming through for you. He's coming through for those of you who are reading this, wherever you may be in the world. He's coming through for you. He's coming through for your family.

Hear this alive word today, a rhema word, a living word: "I will not fail you. I will not abandon you. I will not leave you out in the cold. I will be with you, and I will anoint you to triumph." That's this supernatural era. His presence is manifesting in a fuller measure to reassure you He's with you.

"The battle may be fierce but I'm with you. The situation may look grim, but I'm with you. You will overcome. You will triumph in Christ Jesus." It's a notable deliverance season. Trust Him no matter the trouble.

You may feel like you don't know how you can make it. I didn't know how in the world I could ever make it, but I can testify I did and I can tell you, you can make it too. He will hold your hand; He will not fail. He knows how to set us free.

You don't have to drag this with you anymore. Notable deliverance. Notable, notable, notable, notable. How are you going to make it? Because of Him. Hear Him breathe these words: *"I will not fail you. I will not abandon you. I'm going to take you through this. You're going to pass through the fire. You're not going to be burned."* Your testimony will be "He is the God of notable deliverance."

Reach your hand up to Him. Hold His hand. He's going to take you through.

Hold His hand. Hold to God's unchanging hand. Hold. Hold.

You're walking into notable miracles.

I believe you, just like me, will say, "I don't know how in the world I made it. It had to be Him. He's the God of wonders."

Prayer

Lord, I pray for discouragement and depression, any heavy load, to be lifted off today in Jesus' Name. This is the day freedom comes. I choose to hold Your hand. You know how to set me free and You are faithful to perform it.

26

MOBILIZE ANGELS

We decree the angels of the Lord are bringing our prayers to pass.

In the book of Daniel, Daniel had been praying over the future of his nation and had asked for help and wisdom from God. We are told that God heard Daniel's prayer the very first day that he started praying and had sent one of the most powerful angels, an archangel named Gabriel, with an answer. However, there was spiritual warfare that took place between Heaven and earth in the astrological, or atmospheric, Heaven between Gabriel and a demon prince, the spirit prince of Persia. The battle lasted for 21 days and was quite intense. Here's what the Scripture says concerning Daniel's prayer and the ensuing struggle:

> "Master, listen to us! Master, forgive us! Master, look at us and do something! Master, don't put us off! Your city and your people are named after you: You have a stake in us!" While I was pouring out my heart, baring my sins and the sins of my people Israel, praying my life out before my God, interceding for the holy mountain of my God—while I was absorbed in this praying, the humanlike Gabriel, the one I had seen in an earlier vision, approached me, flying in like a bird about the time of evening worship. He stood before me and said, "Daniel, I have come to make things plain to you" (Daniel 9:19-22 MSG).

Now, try to imagine this. You have prayed for 21 days, and after 21 days of spiritual warfare, Gabriel flies in like a human bird and says, "I'm here to help you. I'm here to answer your prayer."

> "Relax, Daniel," he continued, "don't be afraid. From the moment you decided to humble yourself to receive understanding, your prayer was heard, and I set out to come to you..." (Daniel 10:12 MSG).

Clearly, God assigns angels to bring us answers to prayer. They organize around the prayers of the saints to bring them to pass—especially the prayers of an Ekklesia over a region.

I believe that's why the kingdom of hell fights corporate prayer so intensely. When the Ekklesia gathers in corporate prayer, it mobilizes angels. To change regions or to change a nation often requires angelic assistance, and that is why they have been given to us. Throughout Scripture, we see angels getting people out of trouble in their nations, cities, or in corporate ways, bringing answers to their prayers.

One of the ways you can identify whether you are in a brand-new era in the Kingdom is by fresh anointings of Holy Spirit. Everywhere I go, I see new anointings and outpourings of the Holy Spirit. It's not like it was a few years ago; there's something happening in the atmosphere.

Second, there is increased angel activity. Angels always assist the new eras and new moves of God. Study this in history and you will see angel activity every time. And third, the prophetic words of the apostles and the prophets will declare it. All three of those are happening now in accelerated ways on earth. I've never seen more Kingdom activity in my entire life—it's as if Heaven has amped up, and we need to amp up with it.

Prayer

God, thank You that Your angelic hosts are moving now to bring answers to prayer. We position ourselves to receive Your answer and thank You ahead of time for what You are doing.

27

The Assignment of the Prophetic

We decree prophetic words are intersecting their moment! Now is the time!

Prophetic words are keys to what Holy Spirit is doing, going to do, or wants to do if His people believe and act in faith. They are keys to Christ's Kingdom activity upon the earth and they are keys to angels being released into a region or individuals' lives. Angels really pay close attention to prophetic words. It is amazing to me how many Christians miss the relevance of prophetic words in light of all the Bible says about hearing the prophets and the prophet's reward.

It is very clear prophetic words have an assignment. Isaiah 55:8-11 reminds us of this. God gives them as assignments to be activated by His people individually and His corporate Ekklesia, meaning the prophetic words we've received are mandates from Heaven. It is imperative that they are properly discerned and governed by His written Word. They are assignments for us to grow to completion. It's not going to just automatically happen. It's not based on God's sovereignty. We cannot say, "Well, if God said it, then He is going to do it." No, it has to be acted on by faith just like every promise given in the Scriptures. We have an active part to play. We need to pray, believe, and contend from conception to completion.

God prophesies through Isaiah the prophet, "My words will not come back empty. They will do what I sent them to do. They will complete the assignment I gave them" (see Isaiah 55:11). What's the condition? God's people must engage their faith. It is time for us to do exactly that. When we stand in faith for God's word (prophetic word or dreams) to come to pass, though it may take some time and it usually does, Holy Spirit will lead the Ekklesia to a moment when He can release angels to assist in completing them. He will release favor, power, and strategies. He will supernaturally orchestrate their moment.

In Matthew 1 and Luke 2, we are told the angel Gabriel, the same one that was sent to Daniel, came to Mary with a prophetic promise. The prophetic word from the angel was, "You will have a son and He's going to be named Jesus. He's going to be the Messiah." In fact, Gabriel actually quoted to her the prophet Isaiah's prophecy from Isaiah 7:14 (NKJV): *"The virgin shall conceive and bear a Son, and shall call His name Immanuel."*

Clearly, an angel was paying attention to a prophetic word. He could quote it! He was involved in bringing the word to pass. Many of us have been given prophetic words. Our responsibility is to decree them, pray them, and stand in faith for them and not allow the world or religion to rob us of them. Much of the Church says that is foolishness. No, it's New Testament Christianity and we need to live it. If we will, Holy Spirit will lead us to their time of fulfillment. If we will, angels that are paying attention will help bring them to pass.

Holy Spirit and His angels are paying attention to the prophetic words that we are decreeing. They are paying attention to the prayers we have been praying for years. They are all coming together now. When the New Testament Church does church God's way it intersects a moment. A moment when He can release angels. Our assignment is to keep mobilizing angels with our words.

Prayer

Lord, we say yes to the assignments of the prophetic words You have given to us. Do whatever it takes to get them done. Help us to individually and corporately focus on what You say.

28

The Power Behind Prayer

We decree that prophetic words are coming together now! We decree prayers are coming together now!

Two important areas in which angels assist us are prayer and prophecy. The principle of Scripture is that Holy Spirit sends angels to assist Him in bringing the prayers that we have prayed, the prophetic words we have heard, and prophetic dreams we have received to pass. It's important we see Scripture as a foundation for this.

Let's first look at Holy Spirit and how He sends angels to answer prayers. In Daniel 9 and 10 we see the angel Gabriel was sent to answer Daniel's prayer. Daniel was praying for his nation, about their future, and for wisdom. God heard his prayer as soon as he prayed it and sent Gabriel with the answer. But there was spiritual warfare in the atmospheric heavens by a demon prince, the spirit prince of Persia. This would have been a fallen angel that sided with lucifer when he rebelled and tried to take over Heaven. Lucifer assigned him to govern diabolically, demonically over the area of Persia. This demon prince tried to stop Gabriel, who is not a fallen angel—he is an angel that is still on our side and he's a participant in the Kingdom of God. He is one of God's princes. The spirit prince of Persia tried to stop Gabriel from getting through to answer the prayer, and this battle lasted 21 days.

Angels are sent to answer prayers. God assigns them to bring prayers to pass so there is little wonder that if there is a New Testament church that is actively praying the will of God, believing His prophetic words, and declaring them, He is going to send angels to assist. Angels organize around the prayers of the saints to bring them to pass, especially the Ekklesia's prayers for a region or for a nation. I personally think that's why hell fights prayer so hard, especially corporate prayer of the body of Christ. That is the kind of prayer that mobilizes Angel Armies and the forever loser doesn't want that. To change regions or a nation often requires angelic assistance. Over and over throughout the Word of God we see angels getting involved with nations, people groups, and cities, getting them out of trouble as a result of their prayers and calling out to God.

Angels minister, assist, and God uses them to answer our prayers. The same is true with promises, prophetic words, or prophetic dreams that we are believing for. Holy Spirit activates angels to help bring them to pass.

In our times, the prophetic words are coming together. It's a scriptural pattern. Strategies of good warfare will provide victory after victory. It will be well. The prophetic words have prepared us for the new era. That's what they were about. God is saying this to us—hear it with your spiritual ears. Prophetic words are coming together now. Prayers are coming together now. We will do well. Strategies will be activated through prophetic understanding. Good warfare will be engaged. Prophetic words have prepared the way for a divine shift. What we could not do, God has done through assignments given by prophetic words and the assistance of angels, preparing us for the days ahead.

Prayer

King Jesus, we look to You! Thank You for the angelic help that is assisting our prayers now to see Your Kingdom come and Your will be done on earth. Prepare us for what is to come.

29

He Knows What He Is Doing

We decree that the greatest days in church history are not in our past but in our present and in our future!

Holy Spirit has planned our times well. Lucifer, the forever loser, is not a better planner than Holy Spirit. Not even close! Holy Spirit is a far superior strategist, engineer, and leader than satan ever thought about being. The meticulous detail He is bringing to the days ahead should fill us with hope and confidence. As has always been the case, God knows what He is doing. He has thought it through. It is nonsensical to think the designer of the universe missed something. His brilliance will expose an inferior kingdom of darkness and will reveal God-led plans for His people to win tremendous victories.

Those plans are now unfolding in times He's prepared. Breakthroughs of healings, miracles, resources, and harvests are on the horizon. Hell will not stop Him as He guides the Ekklesia into paths leading into the greatest days in church history. The New Testament Church of Christ's Kingdom will see and live in times Holy Spirit spoke to me about years ago concerning angels saying, "The greatest days in church history are not in your past; they are in your present and your future!" That is His plan and He knows how to do it. Remnant believers in Christ must trust that emphatically and act accordingly. It's time for the radical remnant to follow Holy Spirit to another level.

Revelation for prophetic destiny is similar to putting a puzzle together. You connect one piece to another, and as you do the picture begins to manifest. I believe God does it this way to keep us engaged with Him and from getting ahead of His timing. If He told us everything at once, we might just skip a few things and go straight to the end purpose. It's just human nature. This also allows time to grow our faith. The faith it takes to begin a prophetic journey is usually not enough to finish it. It must keep growing or purpose slows or stagnates. God, in His wisdom, has chosen to grow revelation as we grow our faith.

Again, the prophet Daniel is a great example of this. To understand his times, Daniel went back through the years and read the prophecies concerning the Babylonian captivity. He revisited revelations, visions, dreams, even angel visitations and messages. As he pressed in to seek the Lord with fasting and prayer, the revelation became clear. It's time! It's time for our captivity to end. The 70 years Jeremiah prophesied were ending. They were connecting to their moment.

This understanding enabled Daniel to pray and decree with such bold faith that two of Heaven's strongest angels, Gabriel and Michael, and the divisions of angels they command were sent by Holy Spirit to assist his intercession and bring it to pass.

Amazingly, the prayer of Daniel and God's people crying out for deliverance was answered by Holy Spirit activating two divisions of Angel Armies. This, of course, was done under an old covenant. How much more should this partnership of the Holy Spirit and His Angel Armies, assisting God's very own heirs, function in a new and better covenant—one Jesus established through His Cross. How much more should it operate in Christ's new Kingdom, assisting Christ's very own Ekklesia. Certainly, the bar has been raised. Hell has never faced what Holy Spirit has planned for His true Kingdom.

PRAYER

Holy Spirit, as You prompted Daniel to pray and steward Your Word, draw our attention to words You have spoken so that we may partner in faith to see them come to pass!

30

Planting the Heavens

We decree our words are seeding the atmosphere to bring breakthrough and establish the Kingdom of God!

Jesus taught a lot about planting the heavens with our words. Remember that He first planted the heavens and the earth in Genesis 1. He is the Word. He planted the entire universe with word seed decrees, saying "be" and it was. In Matthew 6:10 (NKJV), He taught us to pray this way, "*Your kingdom come. Your will be done on earth as it is in heaven.*" That's a different kind of prayer because it's not really a petition—it's a declaration. It's not a foretelling of the future—it's a commanding decree. It's calling something to be, calling something to exist. In other words, He said to declare, "Will of God, be done. Will of God, come."

When Jesus walked the earth, we see that His words caused things to happen. Wherever He went, He opened His mouth and He sounded forth decrees that brought miraculous results. In John 6:63 (NKJV) He tells us, "*The words that I speak to you are spirit, and they are life.*" Understand the magnitude of that statement. When Christ spoke, when He opened His mouth and decreed, Holy Spirit moved into the atmosphere. His mouth opened the atmosphere for Holy Spirit to begin to move. Remember, Holy Spirit hovers until He hears the Word of God. When He hears the Word of God declared, He moves, just like He did upon the chaos and darkness in the beginning. Christ's mouth opened ways for the Kingdom to come. His mouth proclaimed an invitation, "Holy Spirit come. Move here."

What Jesus said produced after its kind. The superior reality of the Kingdom of God, a spiritual Kingdom that visibly affects the entire earth, began to move and transform the earth realm. The Word became a reality and produced what He decreed. The seed in the words produced it. Jesus was modeling ministry for you and me, His joint heirs.

When the sons and daughters of God open their mouths and decree God's Word, it can change the atmosphere of a region. Our decrees act as a catalyst that sets in motion a chain of events to bring God's Word to pass. They open the heavens so blessings can rain down, miracles can be produced, and we can receive revelation and enlightenment. Our decrees attract Angel Armies to ascend and descend and assist the heirs of salvation in that region (see Hebrews 1:14).

As God's heirs, as His children on earth, we are commissioned to plant the heavens with His words, to seed them with declarations of truth. We must declare, on the basis of God's Word, the rightful rule of King Jesus over the earth, the region, and over the kingdom of darkness. We are commissioned to do it. It is well past time, but the sons and daughters of God are just waiting for Christ's return, just waiting for Him to come back. We are commanded to occupy until He comes (see Luke 19:13 KJV). We are commanded to rule and reign with Him in this life (see Romans 5:17 KJV). We are to rule over principalities and powers, mights, and dominions of darkness, binding them with superior authority just like Jesus bound them when He opened His mouth and declared that they must go. Sitting silent with closed mouths has never been an option for real heirs.

Prayer

God, wake us up to the reality of what it means to be sons and daughters. Give us boldness to decree and declare what You are saying, to make way for Your mighty presence to come!

31

READY TO MOVE

We decree the King is ready to move!

Psalm 133 describes the season I now believe we are in. Jesus sat down and Father poured the horn that was filled with anointing oil upon His head. This oil ran down off His head, off His beard, and ran down all over His body soaking clear to the outer parts of the body with the heaviest concentration of oil being in His lap.

That's the picture of what happened to Jesus on the first Pentecost in Acts 2. When the king or the high priest would stand up, there would be an extra heavy flow of puddled oil that was in his lap that would flow and splash upon his legs and upon his feet. Please see the prophetic picture.

On the first New Testament Pentecost, Holy Spirit flowed to the Church with the anointing of King Jesus. It was poured out. It ran down and dripped on the waiting body of Christ in the upper room. We no longer have just 120, we have millions and millions of us in the remnant. It occurs in the season of the standing King. It occurs when the King makes His stand. You don't stand unless you are ready to move. The King is ready to move.

In Acts 7, Jesus stands to welcome Stephen into His presence. Stephen had been stoned to death for his passionate witness for Christ. We are now being anointed to run the anchor lap. The last lap of the relay race is called the anchor lap. You save your fastest runners for it. The great cloud of witnesses in Hebrews 12 wants to cheer us on as we run. We are being anointed to run like never before with the

Gospel, and our King Jesus is rising to run before us as Messiah the Breaker to ensure our breakthrough (see Micah 2:13). We are going to break through!

Hear the Word of the Lord:

> "Holy Spirit said we are now entering into the season in which we will shift from Acts 2 to Acts 7. We are moving from the seated King to the standing King who runs before us. In these days the King is going to make another stand, the biggest stand He has ever made upon this earth. He's going to do it through Ekklesias He has been forming. In this season, this Third Great Awakening, this end time surge, the King is going to stand up. The King is going to make His stand to shake the heavens and the earth. He's going to stand and deal with rebel kings. He stands up with His people, He stands to side with His Church in tangible, real ways. When He stands, the anointing that is on Him, the anointing that is in His lap, begins to splash upon the body of Christ. We aren't getting drips, we are getting splashes. It is the season of the gushing flow of the King who makes His stand. When the King stands, the anointing splashes."

For generations oil has been accumulating in the lap of our King. In other words, a portion of all those anointings from previous outpourings of His Spirit has been collected and held in the lap of King Jesus for the season of the standing King, the anointing for the synergy of the ages into the greatest days in church history. The season when He makes His greatest stand.

Prayer

Jesus, we believe we are seeing You stand now. We agree that You are ready to move. Shake the heavens and the earth with Your glorious power so that all will see You are the rightful King!

32

It's Deluge Season

We decree the greatest move of God in history is happening now!

A large portion of the outpouring at Pentecost in Acts 2 has remained in the King's lap, along with all other outpourings. Some of the great Azusa Street outpouring is still in the King's lap. Some of the Cane Ridge outpouring is still in the King's lap. The healing movement—T.L. Osborn, Oral Roberts, Gordon Lindsay, all those healing evangelists—some of that anointing is still in the King's lap. The Moravian revival, the Methodist revival with the Wesleys and Whitefield, the Anglican outpouring with Newton and Wilberforce were all great outpourings and some of that anointing has collected in His lap. It's still there. The great Welsh revival with Evan Roberts that spread through all of Europe—some of that anointing is still in the King's lap. Luther's reformation, still going after 500 years—some of that anointing is still in the King's lap.

The Charismatic Movement, an outpouring that touched millions, was poured out but some of it has collected into the lap of our King. The First Great Awakening in the 1730s and '40s and the Second Great Awakening in the mid-1800s with Charles Finney, Peter Cartwright, Beacher, Moody, Booth, Spurgeon, and Taylor. Some of that outpouring collected in the lap of our King. The Holiness Movement, the great revivalists down through history—Finney, Billy Graham, the Wesleys—anointing for evangelism all collecting and intermingling in His lap for today, for the Third Great Awakening, for the end-time outpouring, and for the synergy of the ages. It's there waiting for the King to make His stand and splash it all over us. It is there to drench the Ekklesias.

Think about this—an Ekklesia, a church, flowing in a portion of all of the other outpourings combined at the same time! Little wonder it's a glorious church. No spots, no wrinkles, and the powers of hell will not prevail against it. All of those moves in and of themselves changed history. What's going to happen when you see them all at the same time? We will be history makers. Our King can do this. His anointing is never wasted. It's just as pure as the day He poured it out. It's just as holy, clean, and pure, waiting for Him to make His stand.

When the King stands, the anointing splashes and the Church is immersed in the synergy of all the outpourings and anointings combined. He has saved a portion of all of it for when He makes His stand. For generations, oil has been accumulating in the lap of our King. Outpouring after outpouring, and now the seated King will become the standing King who sides with us.

This isn't drip season; it's deluge season. It's drench season. Our legs are going to be soaked to run like never before. Our feet are going to be soaked to run with the Gospel of the Kingdom. Heavier glory. Heavier splendor. Heavier presence. Weighty presence. Heavier and heavier anointing. There's never been a move of God on earth like this one. Our King is going to make His stand in visible, clear ways with the Ekklesias. The synergy of the ages is behind this one. The power of the ageless One is behind this one. Angel Armies are behind this one. Holy Spirit is rising in unprecedented ways.

Prayer

Holy Spirit, come. Synergize us together with the greatest move of God in history. Come, King Jesus, and stand with us. Pour fresh oil over us.

33
A New Pentecost

We decree a new Pentecost is anointing us for supernatural acceleration!

Pentecost comes to fill us afresh with a living, breathing God. In a more manifest way, God's life becomes experientially real.

> For you who welcome him, in whom he dwells...you yourself experience life on God's terms (Romans 8:10 MSG).

That's the focus of Pentecost. It's about filling us with Holy Spirit to experience life on God's terms. I don't know about you, but I'm ready for life on God's terms.

> It stands to reason, doesn't it, that if the alive-and-present God who raised Jesus from the dead moves into your life, he'll do the same thing in you that he did in Jesus, bringing you alive to himself? When God lives and breathes in you (and he does, as surely as he did in Jesus), you are delivered from that dead life. With his Spirit living in you, your body will be as alive as Christ's! ... God's Spirit beckons. There are things to do and places to go! (Romans 8:11-14 MSG)

There are gates, doors, and opportunities we are to pass through to new places, inheritances, blessings, and harvests.

> This resurrection life you received from God is not a timid, grave-tending life. It's adventurously expectant, greeting God with a childlike "What's next, Papa?" (Romans 8:15 MSG)

The new-era Pentecost outpouring concerns what comes next on Papa's timeline. Breakthrough is being birthed on this planet through the Ekklesia, and doors are opening into a greater era of intense glory.

> God's Spirit touches our spirits and confirms who we really are. ...And we know we are going to get what's coming to us—an unbelievable inheritance! ...That's why I don't think there's any comparison between the present hard times and the coming good times. The created world itself can hardly wait for what's coming next (Romans 8:16-19 MSG).

An unbelievable inheritance is coming to us. We're going to have confirmed to us more of who we really are, and it's going to be good times, not bad. If God's Word says it is, then it is.

> Everything in creation is being more or less held back. God reins it in until both creation and all the creatures are ready and can be released at the same moment into the glorious times ahead. Meanwhile, the joyful anticipation deepens. All around us we observe a pregnant creation. The difficult times of pain throughout the world are simply birth pangs. But it's not only around us; it's within us. The Spirit of God is arousing us within. We're also feeling the birth pangs. These sterile and barren bodies of ours are yearning for full deliverance. That is why waiting does not diminish us, any more than waiting diminishes a pregnant mother. We are enlarged in the waiting. We, of course, don't see what is enlarging us. But the longer we wait, the larger we become, and the more joyful our expectancy (Romans 8:20-25).

We are being enlarged in the waiting and receiving insight for our times. Our dreams, concepts, visions, and prophetic words are being ripened, and it's breaking open doors for us to run through.

Prayer

Father God, increase the joy of our anticipation as we wait! We wait for You! We expect God and pursue the process.

34
PERSONAL HISTORY

We decree when we are weak, You are strong, and You will not fail us.

Let's look at a time when oppression was strong and long, but God's promise had come to its moment and He acted with great, notable deliverance. It was time for God's people to possess their promised land. After 430 years, the Word of the Lord came to its moment. Israel had already seen 40 years of signs, wonders, miracles, and healings. In fact, it had all started with healing. Every one of them was healed; there wasn't a feeble one among them. Thousands of healings began to be activated.

Some of the greatest words of encouragement in all of the Bible occur in the first part Deuteronomy 31, and they concern a very notable deliverance. They are words from the Almighty God Himself to His people. They are alive with power and hope. The following is my paraphrase of what the Lord says through Moses: "Do not panic before your enemies, no matter who they are, no matter how many there are, no matter their size, because I am personally going before you to lead the way. I will not fail you. I will not abandon you. You should not be discouraged. Do not fear. Take possession of what I promised. Do not listen to demon propaganda saying I will abandon you. I never will. Do not listen to Baal's messenger saying I will fail you. I will personally go before you, and I will not fail you."

Later, God prophesied to His people again through the prophet Isaiah. What a great promise:

> When you pass through the waters, I will be with you; and through the rivers, they shall not overflow you. When you walk through the fire, you shall not be burned, nor shall the flame scorch you (Isaiah 43:2 NKJV).

I like The Message version of this passage:

> When you're in over your head, I'll be there with you. When you're in rough waters, you will not go down. When you're between a rock and a hard place, it won't be a dead end—because I am God, your personal God, The Holy of Israel, your Savior. I paid a huge price for you: all of Egypt, with rich Cush and Seba thrown in! That's how much you mean to me! That's how much I love you! I'd sell off the whole world to get you back, trade the creation just for you (Isaiah 43:2-4 MSG).

Wow, God said, "I'd trade all of creation *just for you.*" His love, His presence gets us over troubled waters. *"Personally, I'll go before you. I'm going to personally see you through."*

Amazing, notable deliverance is now in season, and it's breaking out all over this nation and world, individually and corporately. Some of the most amazing deliverance that has ever been testified to will now happen because He's going to personally see to it.

This promise has come to its moment. And remember, it changes history. This is going to change a lot of your personal history. Many people's personal history has looked like, "This is going to be how it ends." But Alpha says, "*No. That's not how it's going to end. I'd trade all creation to change this for you and I'm going to. I won't fail you. I won't let you down. I won't.*"

Prayer

Father God, thank You that You go before me. Thank You that You are my faithful Leader. I may not know where I'm going, but I know who I'm following. And I trust in You!

35

REROUTING

We declare we are entering into times when miracle after miracle after miracle is beginning to roll.

Change is often needed if miracles are going to come to completion. A change in situations, people, locations, relationships, or even a change in an entire group of people is sometimes needed. To change things sometimes takes time. Miracles aren't always easy to "faith" our way to. There is a fight of faith. A time of standing, and standing is often required while changes needed are made.

So what do you do? You keep on believing and believing because God sees a way. He sees healing that can restore. He sees favoring grace that can turn things around. He sees a rerouting connection. God is an awesome Rerouter. How many times has our God said, "Rerouting!" He sees an answer. He sees a miracle in process.

These principles are true for the Ekklesia Jesus has come to build and establish on earth. They are also true for us in our times. The Church is promised miracles and, yes, some of them are instant. But other miracles grow over time by believing and believing and believing. Some miracles the Ekklesia births must be stood for and they must be fought for by faith over time.

Here at The Oasis where I have pastored for 46 years, we have been believing to see a miracle revival. We have been standing for a transforming miracle to happen in our world, the greatest harvest of souls in history. Our prophets have prophesied a billion-soul harvest is coming. We have been believing for supernatural resources to expand a Kingdom move of God that ushers in the greatest years in church history. We've been believing for big miracles. Huge miracles. Year after year after year we have continued to declare it and believe it. It has been promised by prophetic word after prophetic word time and time again. From its conception we began to pray it and declare it.

There have been setbacks to overcome. Several of them, as a matter of fact, were times when the effort appeared to be dead, and I've felt orphaned a few times and like nothing was happening. Job's comforters have been very vocal, saying, "It's not going to happen, they haven't heard from God, no great move of God is coming, they'll never make it, they are going to go bankrupt and lose everything, no angel came and promised them about the greatest days in church history not being in the past but in the present and in the future. They are hallucinating." But big, region-changing miracles don't happen instantly all the time. Somebody has to keep believing and believing from conception to completion.

PRAYER

Lord, whatever it takes to move us across the Jordan and in to the promise, here we are, Lord—we will do it. We are not those who put our hand on the plow and turn back. We will keep pushing.

36

Growing a Miracle

We declare our persistent faith is making way for miraculous open doors!

At our church, The Oasis, we have contended for miracles for years. Our faith has been stretched and grown. The Lord hasn't missed a thing, and thankfully, the miracle hasn't stopped. God has been working all along. Holy Spirit and His angels have been busy. Yes, there were things that we had to learn particularly regarding Ekklesia. There were changes that had to be made. There was baggage that needed to be removed. There was unbelief that needed to be purged from the camp. There were a couple of Jezebels and Absaloms who have had to be removed.

But for many years we have been growing a miracle, and it will be what God said it will be if we don't faint or become weary in well doing. Will it be different from what we thought? Probably! In fact, obviously, it is simply part of the faith walk. Will it happen in ways we never saw coming? Probably. Will God have to turn some things for good? Obviously! Will it be done through some people we never expected? Probably. Who cares? I just want to be in the middle of it.

It will be done just as it was for Mary, Joseph, and Jesus. Though for 30 years there wasn't much evidence, they were holding on to a promise that did not look possible. For 30 years it didn't look like much was happening. He was a carpenter. Not one miracle, healing, or deliverance. He was supposed to be the Savior of His people, yet no one was saved.

But the miracle hadn't stopped. It was growing to fullness; and when the fullness of time came, when it was ready and mature, suddenly there were miracles everywhere! Blind eyes could see. Deaf ears could hear. Cripples danced. Leprosy was healed. Storms were calmed. Water was walked on. Dead people got up and were raised to life. Bread was multiplied. Miracle after miracle after miracle occurred within the great miracle that grew for 30 years after Christ's birth. That is what we are heading into now.

I believe that God is opening the door to awesome miracles that for years His people have been believing for. He is opening the door for miracles that we have been standing in faith for, even while millions have declared nothing is happening. He is activating great awakening and reformation as promised. One thing is for sure—it is closer than it's ever been. God has been working to activate the greatest miracle, revival, and move of God ever seen. There are now coming miracles, healings, and awesome deliverance. Prodigals will now be coming home and new converts are coming in.

First Thessalonians 5:24 (NASB) says, "*Faithful is He who calls you, and He also will bring it to pass.*" We are going to grow a miracle to completion. That is what we are going to do, and this is the time when we bring it into fullness. You have to keep your eyes on what God said, not on the passage of time.

PRAYER

Lord, You never give a word that You will not bring to pass if we believe from conception to completion. We say what You say, and we stand in faith.

37
Portal of Heaven

We decree God's cavalry will assist us to win great victories.

Angels of enlightenment, or revelation angels, explained matters to people in biblical times, such as Daniel, Abraham, Joshua, Jeremiah, Zechariah, Paul, Peter, and John, to name a few. These angels assisted Holy Spirit in downloading information to John in his book called the Revelation.

These highly trained angels are here right now, and in this new-era decade Holy Spirit is going to use them to activate revelation, enlightenment, instructions, and strategies, just as He did in the Old and New Testaments. They are going to be made available to us at higher levels, connecting the Ekklesia—the government Kingdom of God—to vital information that is beyond the natural realm of understanding.

As heirs, we have a right to special information that angels can connect us to. We have to start opening up to spiritual resources that we have not yet been taking advantage of. We must come into agreement with Kingdom of God principles, or keys, and ask Holy Spirit to activate angels of enlightenment and revelation to come give us that information so we can function at a much higher and wiser level on earth.

We have to normalize what the nominal church and the world consider to be weird Christianity. We need to understand that true Christians and heirs are *supposed* to be assisted by angels. We're *supposed* to be guarded, delivered, strengthened, and connected to resources by them. Angels are *supposed* to assist in battle and set us free. We're *supposed* to be blessed and informed by them. It's in the Bible and we believe it.

It's time to raise the bar and stop living lowered, watered-down Christianity and begin living in Bible reality. Yes, angels assist me. Yes, angels sometimes talk to me and give me messages from Heaven. No, I am never alone. Holy Spirit is always with me and so are His angels. What's odd to me are people who see demons everywhere, hearing devils talking to them all the time. It's weird to listen to the devil and his demons. It's a whole lot smarter to listen to Holy Spirit and the real angels of God. Where in the world did we get so far gone that we think listening to angels is weird, and hearing from demons is *not* weird?

Holy Spirit is saying, "I want you to pray and decree a portal to open over you, releasing the chariots of fire to ascend and descend in your base at a higher level. Decree the heavens open over you, and welcome the cavalry of Heaven's mighty special forces to encamp round about you and to connect with the Ekklesia hubs. Invite them to base their work in your region, and empower them to work through decrees of authority and prayers of faith."

Obviously, this is going to help change the future. We need to declare the portal open for angels of enlightenment to ascend and descend and engage with us, connecting us to supernatural information and understanding, intelligence gathering that we can't do, and secrets, conditions, enemy tactics, and positioning that they are commissioned to communicate to us. This will accelerate a movement that cannot be stopped.

Prayer

Holy Spirit, today I pray You would open a portal of Heaven over me and my household. I invite Your cavalry to work in my home and my region.

38
Chariots of Fire

We decree the chariots of fire are being activated by Holy Spirit to assist the Ekklesia and the new move of God.

When the Ekklesia becomes the King's mouth on earth, declaring what He says, forbidding what He says should be forbidden and permitting what He wants permitted, we are going to see the chariots of fire, mighty warriors of Heaven, come to our aid and defense. We will see the King's cavalry engage with us in ways that have not been seen for centuries. We are about to see the weapons of our warfare that have been reserved for an operational Ekklesia. Information will be revealed, enabling us to release decrees that need to be decreed. We have entered into the God-planned season of spiritual whirlwinds and chariots of fire in the hands of Heaven's warriors, coming to assist the transition of ministers and ministries and the promotion of servants. Indeed, apostolic chiefs are now rising and a division of angels called "Chariots of Fire" is going to back them.

Where is the God of Elijah? Where is the God of Abraham, Isaac, Jacob, Peter, James, John, and the Apostle Paul? The world is about to find out where He is! God is in the midst of His glorious Ekklesia, just as He said He was going to be, making His stand with them. When God says He is going to have a glorious Ekklesia, He means it, and He is moving divisions of angels into place to assist. It is happening now, and we have to discern what's going on.

Just as Elijah's servant, we also sometimes think the numbers are too low. But not if you recognize there's a Spirit realm with plenty of angelic warriors. As heirs of God and joint heirs with Christ, we are not helpless. We need to discern our times so we can function as Christ defined us. We have not done that yet, but we will so we can operate in the real authority of the spiritual Kingdom of God, affecting the natural kingdoms of the earth.

Holy Spirit affirmed all these thoughts to me as I was watching a special documentary concerning the great war fighters of the United States who were helping to fight terrorism in Afghanistan. An Afghan general was interviewed and asked if he had a problem with our troops being on their base. He simply replied, "Oh no, not a problem at all. We welcome the greatest war fighters on the earth. We welcome them."

When the general said that, I heard Holy Spirit say to me: "You need to welcome the greatest cavalry to your base. You need to welcome the greatest war fighters, the greatest warriors in the universe, to your apostolic base. If you will, they will guard you from hell's terrorism and protect the awakening and the harvest of the ages that I have assigned to you." Please know we have awesome, fierce warriors available to share our apostolic and prophetic bases with us. We need to welcome them and release them with decrees of faith that Holy Spirit prompts inside us.

PRAYER

Thank You, Lord, that Your strategies always win. Hell's strategies will lose. Our hope is in You.

39

STRIKE MISSION

We decree You are staging things right now to bring great triumph, victory, and the great harvest.

Hear what Holy Spirit is saying about our times:

"I am now releasing My mighty ones to break up entrenched evil. They will strike the forever loser's protection of diabolical root systems in America's capital and in the state capitals. Michael, My war prince, has released, in sufficient numbers, war angels to unlock this nation and break barrier walls.

"Companies of our special forces—the angels of fire—have penetrated realms of iniquity and will now destroy them. Cover-ups will be uncovered. Giants, taunting in opposition, will fall. Strongholds of darkness will be destroyed and their influence shattered off territories, regions, and nations.

"My angels are merging with My people to break the forces of evil from Baal's government. My unshakable Kingdom will rise in waves of power, enforcing realignment to My covenant roots. Hear the sounds of battering rams of My Kingdom, resounding against wicked strategies. The abominations will not stand, for overwhelming might will now come to bear upon covenant breakers that seek to destroy My purpose.

"The advance of My Kingdom will be rapid. Rapid strikes will come against hindering spirits, spirits of perversion, government tyranny, and cultural systems polluted by demons. The world will now see the mobilizing of My Kingdom Ekklesia and Heaven's Angel Armies under Lord Sabaoth.

"This will suddenly and aggressively be revealed. It will see the fierceness of hell's resistance of My Kingdom superseded by the fierceness of My wrath against their allegiance to Baal. My fierce deployment will now engage; the saints will engage; My Church will engage. My intercessors are willing and will deploy on strike missions against hell's dominions in ways and in numbers never seen before. My word, their word. My word will fuel the angels who are harkening to assist them. The deployment begins.

"A very fierce war season is now beginning. Engage and win it with My power through prayer, decrees of faith, and worship warfare. Know this, an agitated demon realm will stir violence in the natural realm. But I will send fresh power from Heaven and it will resource you. Fresh fire will be seen of My manifest presence, and I will hover over you in manifest glory, radiating continued support, as I did for My people in the Exodus. Behold and know that I have now opened a door of Heaven. I have opened the angel gate. I have opened the war gate. I have opened the door of Angel Armies to the King's Ekklesia.

"They will now deploy on strike missions, for I will have My harvest. Answers are now going to rain down. Answers are raining down on the Ekklesia. Answers are raining down in all states and in nations. A supernatural time is being launched."

We, the Ekklesia, must come into agreement with this and declare what He's saying. What is all this concerning? The battle is for the throne: Who's going to lead? Who's going to sit on the throne of the nation? Who's going to take their seat? Is Jesus going to be exalted as Lord? (Spoiler alert: Yes, He is!)

Holy Spirit is staging things right now to bring great triumph to King Jesus. The campaign is on to bring Him triumph, and He's not going to back down; He's not going to stop. He is staging things right now for the great victory, for the great harvest.

Prayer

Jesus, we ask You to draw every heart to You and release revival and awakening in our nation. May Your Name be exalted in all the earth, above every other name.

40
SPIRIT LANGUAGE

We decree Holy Spirit is tearing down strongholds.

The baptism of the Holy Spirit that Jesus commanded believers to receive is far more than most have ever even thought about. Praying in other tongues as Holy Spirit gives utterance is authority language that is loosed upon earth once again through sons and daughters. It's God's wisdom or often His strategies being prayed upon the earth. Sometimes, praying in the Spirit could concern God's judgment or His forbidding or releasing of things on earth, using His heirs as the Dominion Mandate originally intended. Sometimes, Holy Spirit, through us, comes against a throne of iniquity or darkness or some activity of hell's kingdom.

There are times, when I'm praying in the Spirit, that revelation surges and an awareness dawns in my spirit, and I find myself decreeing things, such as, "Power of darkness, you're coming down. Throne of iniquity, you will not stand. You're bound and forbidden. The power of Heaven is coming against you today and you're going to be scattered and shattered. Your stronghold is broken. Angels are being released to battle and you're going to lose. This battle is the Lord's. The Kingdom of God is going to occupy the throne." Those types of decrees rise up out of my spirit quite often when I begin to govern in Spirit language.

I know that sounds foreign to much of the Church today, but it is New Testament Christianity. There are times when praying in my spirit language that I have known I am partnering with the Holy Spirit to pull down strongholds. He's praying through me to assist the binding of some kind of work of darkness. Actually, I have probably been praying with hundreds of other intercessors, agreeing together against the enemy. My weapon isn't a natural flesh weapon, it is a spiritual, supernatural, Kingdom of God weapon of governing intercession.

Paul said to the Corinthian Ekklesia in 2 Corinthians:

> For though we walk (live) in the flesh, we are not carrying on our warfare according to the flesh and using mere human weapons. For the weapons of our warfare are not physical [weapons of flesh and blood], but they are mighty before God for the overthrow and destruction of strongholds (2 Corinthians 10:3-4 AMPC).

King Jesus does expect His Ekklesia to make a stand against cultural and societal issues in the world, and one of the keys, tools, or weapons we are to use is praying in the Spirit. Speaking in other tongues as the Spirit gives utterance is one of my best weapons. I intend to use the smashing power of releasing Spirit language. According to Jesus, in John 16:7, it gives me the advantage in spiritual warfare. Being filled with the Spirit and praying in the language of the Spirit gives the saints the advantage and we prevail.

Prayer

Holy Spirit, baptize me with Your fire today. Bring Spirit utterance out of my heart to pray as You pray.

41

Supernatural Boldness

We decree an anointing of boldness is rising in the body of Christ.

This will be an age of supernatural boldness. I received this dream from Gina Gholston, a prophetic dreamer from Clarksville, Tennessee, concerning boldness:

> I just returned from Billye Brim's prayer conference in Branson, Missouri. I opened my Facebook tonight and saw that you, Dutch, and Ken Malone were having meetings in Florida and that the conference was called the Backbone Summit. My jaw dropped when I read this title because I was immediately reminded of a dream I had on March 30, 2019. In this dream, I was standing in an operating room. I saw in front of me an operating table, but at the head of the bed where the pillow should have been was a hole, and that struck me as odd. I knew it was set up like this for a purpose.
>
> As I was looking at that operating table, two men came in through the door holding up and leading a man into the OR. The man looked old and decrepit and was in major pain. He was grimacing and his body was shaking from pain and agony. He had on regular clothes, jeans and a shirt. They led him to and laid him on this operating table face down. His face was positioned in the hole where the pillow should have been.

I then noticed that his shirt did not have a back on it. His back was exposed, but instead of a normal back, there was a huge gaping wound from his neck down to his hips. As I looked at that wound, I saw that he did not have a backbone. It was as if it had been removed and he was left with the agony of the effects of that open wound and spineless condition.

I then noticed the two men who brought him into the OR had left the room, but the doors opened again and they came back in, carrying a brand-new backbone. It was a real skeletal backbone. I knew this was why we were in this OR. This was what all this had been for. They were giving this man a backbone.

They took the new backbone and placed it in the opening on the man's back. When they did, the wound was immediately healed and the man stood up straight and tall and walked out the doors. He was not old and decrepit as he had initially appeared. He was a young man. He was instantly strong and vibrant. He was renewed, restored, revolutionized. He had received a backbone.

A few days later, the Lord said to Gina, "My Church has appeared to be old and decrepit, fallen into ruin and disrepair, but I have brought you to a season of restoration. I have prepared this moment. I have put a backbone in My Church, My Ekklesia, and they will stand up straight, strong, vital, courageous, and revolutionized. This will change everything."

What a glorious moment we are in. God has led us to a Holy Spirit-planned moment, and He is strengthening His body to stand in power, with courage, and display a new backbone. We will advance and prevail.

Prayer

Holy Spirit, help Your Ekklesia recognize the supernatural season we are in and advance forward with boldness and passion. Anoint us with great courage for the hour we are in.

42

DEFINITION TO HISTORY

We decree revelation of Your Word is equipping and empowering us to walk in Your validation and our authority as believers.

Don't underestimate this moment and its ability to change places, nations, and history. It's one aspect of the supernatural era that Holy Spirit has been preparing for over a decade. Scripture promises are in their due time. Hundreds of them, probably better stated thousands of them, have come into that connective, due season moment.

Dreams, visions, and prophecies have come into a *kairos* moment. Scriptures that we have taught, decreed, prayed, and declared now make history. Jesus Himself is now going to oversee and work to cause those Scriptures to come to pass. Holy Spirit has already sent Angel Armies to assist in their arrival.

God's words that we have proclaimed will now change history. Why? Because they have connected to a moment and it is now time for the Godhead to act. In other words, there will be times when what you just heard of God's Word is going to come true right in front of your eyes.

The declarations of promises in God's Word that we've been making for more than a decade will now make history in His Ekklesia. They are all now being connected supernaturally into this moment. As the Godhead determines, it's our time to act. Our King will take center stage with scrolls of God's Word in His hands, just as He did at the temple. We have prayed and planted those words and we have watered them with our tears. But now they are in a designated moment which changes everything as they activate to make new history. It's why the prophets and apostles always say, *You are in the time when history is made and history will change.*

Jesus is stepping forward with His heirs to activate their true definitions in this place and in hundreds of others. I believe that's what part of this healing movement is about. That's why we encourage all Ekklesias to be part of this. Jesus, His Holy Spirit, and angels are going to cause places that have stood and declared the Word of God to come alive and change history in those regions.

Our God is going to shine in this moment in ways that have not been seen before, at least in the magnitude they are now going to be seen, as He begins to reveal more of His glory. There will be a greater weight of His presence. This is the Godhead's plan and vision for the Ekklesias of the world. God's Word will not return to Him void. It will not. God's Word will not be seen as weak or ineffective. In all Ekklesias that have declared His Word without compromise, energizing power is coming to cause the Scriptures they've stood for to change history.

The overwhelming power of God's Word will reform our times, our society, our culture, and our governments. God's Word will bring definition to history. The world is without definition right now. It can't define anything. It can't define a woman. It can't define truth. The King and His Church are rising to oversee great changes.

God is rising to bring definition back into the world based on His Word and His truth, not upon the ignorance of fallen humanity. We are moving into the times of the King's validations upon His heirs, upon the true Ekklesia. I believe that it's now connected to its moment and we are not just speaking prophetically at this point; we are activating into the nations what has been spoken.

Prayer

Lord, we believe we are in the season when You will rise and You will shine. Remove any hindrance or obstacle for this to happen. Release Your angels to clear the way for how You are revealing Yourself in this hour.

43

ACTIVATING RHEMA WORDS

We decree prophetic words that are infused with God-assignments are intersecting their moment right now.

Isaiah 55 is a prophetic word given by God through Isaiah the prophet. It is important to understand that this is a prophetic word. Please note the wording God uses in verse 11: "[Prophetic words will] *do the work I send them to do, they'll complete the assignment I gave them*" (Isaiah 55:11 MSG). Prophetic words have assignments. For example, Mary, the mother of Jesus, asked the angel Gabriel, "How can I have a son by immaculate conception? How is that possible?" Amazingly, Gabriel actually quoted to her a prophecy that is recorded in Isaiah 7:14 (NKJV): "*...the virgin shall conceive and bear a Son, and shall call His name Immanuel.*" Clearly angels pay attention to prophetic words and their assignments.

Then Gabriel said to Mary, "With God nothing is impossible" (see Luke 1:37). The Greek word used is *rhema*—no *rhema* is impossible with God. It means a word that God speaks fresh to us. It is a word of promise that Holy Spirit breathes fresh anointing on, causing that word to come alive and you know it is from His written Word—a word He is speaking directly to me.

Rhema is Holy Spirit-made-alive words that activate to produce when you stand for that word in faith. Faith is always an active ingredient within it. Gabriel says literally, "No *rhema* word is impossible."

Impossible is *adunateo,* the Greek word for impotent, weak, or unable. So this great archangel says, "Mary, nothing God says or promises to you is impotent. Nothing He prophesies is weak. It will produce."

In essence, God says in this prophetic (*rhema*) word through Isaiah, "The word that I give to you will not return empty. It will do what I want it to do. It will accomplish what I determine it to accomplish. My words to you, My prophetic words to you, My promises to you will complete the assignments I gave to them."

We need to recognize that prophetic words and *rhema* words have an assignment on them. God gives them as assignments to be activated by His people, His Kingdom, an Ekklesia, a nation, a New Testament church. A prophetic word to us is an assignment for us to grow to completion. We are to believe that word from conception to completion.

It does not automatically happen because it is not based on God's sovereignty. In other words we can't say, "Well God said it so it's going to happen." No, it has to be acted on by faith. It has to be stood for, believed, fought for, and prayed for from conception to completion.

The prophetic (*rhema*) word has a God-assignment on it that simultaneously gives the Ekklesia, the New Testament church, an assignment as well. When we hear a word of the Lord, it assigns something to us that we must decree, pray, and strategize with Holy Spirit about and implement. We must engage with Angel Armies that are activated to assist it. It simultaneously gives the apostles, the saints, and you an assignment. When we engage with the *rhema* word, potent power of Holy Spirit begins to activate supernaturally to do what He wants done.

Remember what the apostle Paul told his spiritual son Timothy. Prophetic words are strategies for good warfare: "*This charge I commit to you, son Timothy, according to the prophecies previously made concerning you, that by them you may wage the good warfare*" (1 Timothy 1:18 NKJV).

Prayer

Holy Spirit, remind us of the words You have spoken that need to be contended for and grown. Help us wage war with the words of Your heart for our season, our families, our cities. May Your words come and bear fruit now!

44
THE DOMINION MANDATE

We decree we are filled with the King's speech and nations will know our King.

Genesis 1:26-28 is commonly called the *Dominion Mandate*. God gave a divine purpose to man from the very beginning of creation. He commissioned man by saying, "You are here to be fruitful, multiply, and subdue the earth and have dominion over everything in it." It is highly significant that the first thing God said to Adam and Eve was, "I want you to rule the earth for Me. I am authorizing you to govern. Societies will need government. See to it. Plant My Word everywhere and dominion will be activated."

It was God's will for His imaged ones to rule and reign on earth. That was His original intent, and you must understand what this means if you are ever going to clearly understand purpose. Why? Because hell has done everything it can to distort God's purpose so that hell's kingdom, not God's Kingdom, can rule the earth.

Christ's death and resurrection reactivated God's original intent for His born-again children. He restored lost purpose and purposes, and He reactivated the Dominion Mandate. No purpose of God can ultimately fail. It may become disrupted, but it is going to resurrect and the purpose of God will always be done.

Jesus came and redeemed us from the fall of man in Genesis. He restored us back to God and clothed us in His righteousness. When

Christ rose from the dead, having finished the sacrifice for man's redemption, He repeated the same words that the Godhead originally spoke to man in the beginning. In Matthew 28:18 (NKJV), He arose from the dead saying, *"All authority has been given to Me in heaven and on earth."* In other words, "Now you reign in My Name. All authority has been given to me. I delegate it to you—now you rule. You reign. You govern. You have dominion." He commanded us, "You, disciple nations. Become My Kingdom government upon the earth."

In Romans 5:17, the apostle Paul said that we are to reign in life through Jesus Christ. Clearly, God wanted the earth filled with those made in His image who would bring the earth under the influence of His Kingdom. He wanted a Kingdom. He wanted His sons and His daughters ruling with Him, walking in right relationship with Him, and exercising their delegated authority on earth. Even though I believe that Jesus is coming and we will be taken out of here at some point, an escape mentality stops us from occupying or taking care of God's business until He comes. We have conveniently suppressed the truth, thus empowering hell's kingdom to rule the nations, territories, and lands in our place. We are giving up our gardens just as surely as Adam and Eve gave up theirs, and it is time for it to stop. All of creation is crying out for it to stop.

It's time to rule and reign with Christ in this life, governing by declaring, cultivating, and making a stand for God's Word. It's time for the New Testament Church and remnant believers to arise and say what God says. That is how we rule. It's time to raise our voices, shake off deadly passivity, and fulfill the Dominion Mandate God has given us. The world is meant to be discipled by the sons and daughters of God who realize and use their authority in Jesus' Name.

PRAYER

King Jesus, we know it's time for Your Church to rule and reign. Grant us clarity and align us to see ourselves as Your sons and daughters. Activate our authority in Jesus' Name!

45
GREATER IN NUMBER

We decree You anoint us with power from Heaven and the same works Jesus did, the same healings and miracles, will manifest now all around the world.

The words Jesus spoke to His disciples the night of the Last Supper are also words to all believers. Jesus told them it was time for Him to leave but that He would come again. He looked around the table and began to teach. In John 14:12-14, He made what I believe is one of His most astounding statements.

> I tell you this timeless truth: The person who follows me in faith, believing in me, will do the same mighty miracles that I do—even greater miracles than these because I go to be with my Father! For I will do whatever you ask me to do when you ask me in my name. And that is how the Son will show what the Father is really like and bring glory to him. Ask me anything in my name, and I will do it for you! (John 14:12-14 TPT)

If it's timeless, it's true today. This Scripture says *"greater miracles,"* meaning greater in number, not greater in quality. Jesus did signs, wonders, and miracles in a relatively small area: Israel and its surrounding regions. But we are involved in the whole world. We're involved in a Kingdom revival. We need far more, greater in number, signs, wonders, and miracles because of the size and the scope of our assignment into all the world.

In the book of Acts, the leaders of the dead religion tried to intimidate Peter and John after a notable miracle. And then they persuaded the government of the times to issue a decree to Peter and John that said, "We forbid you to ever do this again, and do not even preach in the name of Jesus." To which Peter and John said, and I'm paraphrasing, "Go pound sand. You can't intimidate us. We'll do exactly what our King told us to do. We'll not be silent. He told us to speak in His name and He told us to do miracles in His Name."

The council got together, wondering what they could do about this. Acts 4:15 says:

> But when they had commanded them to go aside out of the council, they conferred among themselves, saying, "What shall we do to these men? For, indeed, that a notable miracle has been done through them is evident to all who dwell in Jerusalem, and we cannot deny it" (Acts 4:15-16 NKJV).

Sadly, much of the Church has become stagnant because it has settled for the natural, and it has dispensationalized the supernatural. But the remnant that has been prepared for our times, the remnant in the true Church, the King's Ekklesia, is refusing to settle for the natural realm way of doing things. Like Peter and John, the remnant will refuse to bow their knee to the fear of man. Instead, this generation reserved for this age will passionately follow their King.

Prayer

Our King, we pledge our allegiance to You. We'll follow Your Spirit, with our eyes locked on You. No measure of intimidation will diminish our loyalty and love for You.

46

MESSIAH THE BREAKER

We decree we are entering the seasons of supernatural breakthrough.

I've seen all types of breakthrough in my life over the years. There have been times when the Lord just simply broke things up and I was free. He busted confinement with the various means of His power at His disposal and I passed through.

There have been plenty of other breakthroughs where the Holy Spirit has helped me grow my way through. I had to strengthen myself in the spirit, growing my faith, getting rid of any areas of unbelief or any issues that I needed to, and then He led me to the doors of breakthrough.

Some breakthroughs have resulted in God impregnating my soul with possibilities, dreams, ideas, concepts, callings, and prophecies. All seeds have different gestation periods. For a woman, it is nine months. If you're raising tomatoes, you can get a crop in a few weeks, but if you're growing an oak tree, it's going to take a few years.

In the spiritual realm, some dreams have a longer gestation period than others. There have been many times breakthroughs that God has given have come through, impregnating my soul with possibilities and dreams that I've had to nourish, feed, and protect until it was time for it to break through and live on the earth. Other times I had to raise dreams like you would raise a child.

Micah 2:13 says God will burst all confinements. It is the season for confinement to break as Messiah the Breaker goes before us as

His Kingdom advances. The confinements and constraints upon the Church are now going to be supernaturally broken. Millions of promises will now spring up and break free—no more confinement and no more delay. The breaker angels accompanying Him have heard the King's decree to break confinement. When we stop listening with our natural ears to what the world is saying and start listening with our spiritual ears, we will hear the chains of disease, poverty, fear, bondage, and depression break.

> The Breaker [the Messiah] will go up before them. They will break through, pass in through the gate and go out through it, and their King will pass on before them, the Lord at their head (Micah 2:13 AMPC).

Alah is the Hebrew word for *go up* and is used over 900 times in the Old Testament (Strong's H5927). *Alah* also means "to go from a lower elevation to a higher one." It pictures, in the Hebrew language, sheep being led by their shepherd to a higher feeding area. *Alah* compares to *anago*, which is the Greek word for *led up*. *Anago* also means "to mount up, rise up, or to go to a higher elevation" (Strong's G321). In Matthew 4:1, we read that Jesus was *led up* by the Holy Spirit to a mountain, where He fasted and prayed for 40 days, overcoming the devil's attack. Both Micah 2:13 and Matthew 4:1 are describing Jesus the Messiah. In the Old and the New Testaments, Messiah the Breaker is described as one who takes sheep to a higher level.

Anago and *alah* give clear prophetic meaning to us today. The identity of Messiah the Breaker prophesies to us that He will give breakthrough after breakthrough so that we can go to higher and higher levels in life, relationships, purpose, and ministry. There is a remnant with a willingness to follow the Breaker and go up to advance Christ's Kingdom to a new level on the earth.

PRAYER

God, thank You that You are restoring clear vision across Your Ekklesia, leading us into the greatest harvest we have ever seen, confirmed by signs, wonders, and miracles.

47

THE KINGDOM SURGE

We decree it's time for the synergy of the ages. It's time for the divine convergence of the ages. It's time for the greatest days in church history.

A worldwide revival is beginning to roll through America and the world. It will be, I believe, like the snowball getting bigger and bigger until finally it's going to roll right over the gates of hell. It's going to steamroll demon strongholds. It's going to scatter, shatter, and roll over antichrist governing systems. It's going to roll right through demonic, cultural, and societal hinderances. We are living in awesome times because we have now entered into the days of Christ's Kingdom surge. It's going to move through this world in ways never thought possible before.

The Church is now going to do some brand-new things in some new ways, and hell will now face a New Testament Church it has never faced before. One that is based on the foundation of the apostles and the prophets, and it will be the Church functioning in Kingdom of God governing authority right here and right now. There has never been a Kingdom move of God like this Third Great Awakening.

I know that is a big statement but I absolutely believe it. There has never been anything like what I am seeing in all of church history. From glory to glory to glory must somehow mean bigger and bigger and bigger; greater and greater and greater; stronger and stronger and stronger; more powerful, more powerful, and more powerful. It cannot mean weaker and weaker and weaker until Christ finally comes back to save us. Like the three Hebrew boys, this Church isn't going to bow to its enemies.

One tremendous aspect of this new era is the converging of the ages. Holy Spirit has been planning the supernatural convergence of the ages for years. It is coming to pass in our times. This is highly significant. I believe that is why the revelation of Angel Armies was given to me. We need angels for the convergence of the ages. We need them to assist this awesome move of God. We need angels to help us overcome hell's strongholds, tear down demonic thrones in regions, and help with the harvest. Jesus said angels assist His Kingdom as harvesters and reapers. You can see that in Matthew 13:39. Angels do all of this, and they do so much more. Holy Spirit knows this, and He has begun to supervise the release of millions and millions of angels upon this planet.

When Holy Spirit began to reveal Angel Armies to me, it prompted years of study and a journey I am still on today. Holy Spirit began to download revelation about how angels assist us, and He showed me the convergence of the ages. He also revealed to me that King Jesus had issued an order for a new campaign upon the earth, greater than the outpouring in Acts 2. He was coming to supervise and empower a fresh outpouring of the Holy Spirit coming upon this earth. A new Pentecost would now be released and revival would spread everywhere on the planet. It would not be a local church revival that is only in a few places. This would be a Kingdom revival that is everywhere.

Prayer

God, we ready ourselves for the Kingdom revival that is now here. Release Your presence to move and ignite a new Pentecost here and now!

48

THE ANGEL GATE

We decree the angel gate has been opened and there are more with us than against us.

It wasn't so long ago that many Christians didn't know or understand faith decrees or the meaning and function of an Ekklesia, and many still aren't aware. But now there is rising an Ekklesia with a better understanding of ruling and reigning and how to decree their faith and authority. The Godhead has released Angel Armies in unprecedented numbers; the angel gate is open! I have not seen any other time in history that has the vast number of angels deployed in it as what is happening right now.

The Godhead, with its deployment of angels, is helping a willing remnant to cleanse the spirit realms and to dethrone demon principalities and powers, preparing for what we have been told is a billion-soul harvest, through a great shaking and a reset of our covenant roots in America. When Holy Spirit began downloading a deeper understanding of Angel Armies to me, He spoke two things that I've held on to ever since. He said, "The greatest days in church history are not in your past; they are in your present and in your future," and, "I will now lead another campaign for King Jesus, similar to Acts 2; only this time, I will be bringing far more of the Angel Armies." I believe that campaign has begun and we are going to live out what we have been stewarding for years.

Angels do not do their own bidding. They are under the authority of their leader, as we are told in Colossians 2:9-10 (ESV): *"For in him the whole fullness of deity dwells bodily, and you have been filled in him, who is the head of all rule and authority."*

Who is the head of all rule and authority? Jesus! We don't have any problem with that; of course He is their Leader. And so is Holy Spirit, because Jesus said that Holy Spirit was His other self:

> And I will pray the Father, and he shall give you another Comforter, that he may abide with you for ever (John 14:16 KJV).

The Greek word for *another* is *allos*, which means "another of the very same kind" (Strong's G243). Jesus was saying that He will give us another comforter (*allos*), one of the same kind as Him. "My other Me" would be another way to translate that. Holy Spirit is equally part of the Godhead—just as Jesus and the Father—therefore, He is the Head of all principalities, rulers of darkness, thrones, and dominions. He has supreme authority over all angels, both the fallen ones and the good ones.

The King's Ekklesia is to exercise authority that has been delegated to them, and they are to bind, remove, take down, and stop the evil influences and sit over that region themselves. It's to be a seat where the Ekklesia sits in Christ's authority and His Name. It is the Ekklesia who should influence the territory, the region, and the nation with what God says, stewarding it with biblical principles. We are to dethrone hell's leadership in spirit realms that are affecting natural realms. To do that, we must pray and decree our authority in Christ's Name.

Prayer

Holy Spirit, may Your Church rise up now in greater authority! Infuse us with boldness now! Fill us with Your Spirit so that Your leadership would be on the throne in our lives, our homes, our regions.

49

Completing a Dream

We declare supernatural recoveries for past losses, finding us and resourcing us.

And Joseph dreamed a dream... (Genesis 37:5 KJV).

Beginning in Genesis 37, we see how Jacob's son, Joseph, grew a God-dream. Joseph's dream occurred over time. The prophetic dream happened, but it didn't happen instantly. When Joseph was 17 years old, he was thrown into a pit by his brothers and sold into slavery because they did not like his dream. Joseph was sold to Potiphar's house where God anointed him with great favor and he began to learn very important management skills. That was great for a while, but it didn't look like it was moving him toward his dream. In fact it looked just the opposite. It looked like his dream was over.

Joseph was falsely accused of rape and was thrown into prison, but once again God opened a door for him. He began to learn to manage that prison; and as a result, God opened a door to Pharaoh's household. Pharaoh himself had a dream and needed the dream interpreted. When no one else could interpret the dream, Joseph was remembered as one who interpreted dreams, and he was called to the palace where he interpreted the dream for Pharaoh. This began to open the door for Joseph's own dream, years before, to take place. God had told Joseph in his dream, "You will even have authority over your own household." God was miraculously moving him from prison to palace.

Joseph was in captivity for 13 years—nearly half of his life to that point. It looked like nothing was happening, as if the dream was never going to take place. However, we know that plenty was happening; it just wasn't visible to Joseph. It looked to Joseph like the dream had died 13 years before, but God was working. Think about what God had to do to complete Joseph's dream. A major move had to take place in order for the dream to be realized. God had to move him to another country, in this case Egypt. Joseph needed to learn stewardship, accounting, and management skills. Because Joseph was the youngest of Jacob's sons, he wasn't going to have the opportunity to learn these skills at his father's house.

It was necessary for people to be moved in and out of Joseph's life in order for the dream to begin to unfold. The most powerful man in government of that time, Pharaoh, had to come into power and then God had to prepare him to accept Joseph who was not only from another country but was actually a slave.

Weather patterns had to be changed to bring about the seven years of plenty. Think about that. The weather patterns of the entire earth had to be changed for Joseph's dream to be accomplished and then they had to be shifted again for seven years so that his declaration of seven years of plenty and seven years of famine could come to pass.

The hearts of Joseph's brothers, who deposed him, had to be changed, and this would take some time. The dream didn't happen instantly. For 13 years it looked like the miracle would never happen. To Joseph the dream appeared dead; to God it looked like it was going to happen. Even though to Joseph it appeared to be dead, all kinds of things were happening! God was changing an entire nation, its government, and weather patterns to accommodate His dream to a man. It grew to completion. Joseph's part in it was to believe even when he could see nothing happening.

PRAYER

Lord, we invite You to take us to a new level and a new season spawning miracle after miracle after miracle. Help us see You in the middle as the dream is growing.

50

RE-VIVE-ALL

We decree re-vive-all angels are assisting Holy Spirit in breathing fresh life into God's people.

On February 14, 2019, I began to see, in the spirit realm, extremely strong winds blowing from the four corners of the earth. Remember Ezekiel had prophesied in Ezekiel 37:9 (KJV): "...*Come from the four winds, O breath, and breathe upon these slain, that they may live.*" The Contemporary English Version reads, "*Blow from every direction.*"

The words *breath* and *spirit*, used interchangeably throughout the text, are translated from the Hebrew word *ruwach* (Strong's H7307). Holy Spirit is the *ruwach* of God. He's the Breath Spirit that entered the lifeless skeletons, causing them to come alive.

In my vision, Holy Spirit was blowing life from all directions and I could see thousands of angels riding upon those four winds. They looked to me like flying clouds of angels, just as thousands of birds look like in the winter when they flock together so densely that they look like a flying bird cloud. I began to pray, "God, what are You showing me? Give me understanding." In my spirit, I heard Holy Spirit say, "This is a division of angels now being released for the new days."

Over the next several days, I continued praying and asking, "Lord, who are they? Show me; what do they do?" At the end of five days, something happened to me that has never occurred before. On Monday, February 18, I began to hear and see one word, over and over, all week long. The word was *revival,* but it was spelled differently. The word I saw was *re-vive-all.*

In my spirit I heard the word "re-vive-all" echoing over and over. I even thought I heard it spoken out loud. During this time, Holy Spirit began to download information to me concerning this word signifying a division of Angel Armies. I knew that this was about the magnificent revival that has been prophesied for decades.

Re-vive-all angels are being deployed on Holy Spirit winds. They are being activated and are riding Breath Spirit's wind into all the earth.

Holy Spirit is answering our prayers by deploying millions of angels to revive us, to reinvigorate the bride and fill their lamps with oil. The outpouring is a replenishing one, so the bride can take all she needs—there will be plenty more. The fresh winds of revival are blowing. I believe these revival angels are assisting Holy Spirit in the times of refreshing referred to in Acts 3:20.

Many of us have been through what seem to be times of desert heat, bleaching us to the bone. We've endured hot times when we've felt very dry, when it seemed our hope was gone and there was nothing left. We've seen our visions strewn about and disconnected in the desert valleys. We've been picked clean by opportunistic demon vultures, while satanic wolves have scattered our bones every which way. But Breath Spirit says the bones can live. Breath Spirit says, "Watch this. I'm bringing the breath of life to you and you'll come to life."

Re-vive-all angels are assisting Holy Spirit in breathing fresh life into God's people. They are aiding Holy Spirit strategy in strengthening and encouraging the remnant. No matter what the circumstance, no matter your condition, you can be revived.

PRAYER

Lord Jesus, breathe on us again today. Where refreshment is needed, come with Your wind. We welcome Your re-vive-all angels!

51

A Divine Turnaround

We decree that every word of God is true and we will be provided for by the dream's promises.

The dreams of our churches and individual lives can now be realized because the efforts of our God over time are now converging. They are converging into this season to begin to fulfill dreams that His people have had for years. It may appear that nothing has been happening, but we keep believing. God may have had to move all kinds of things in order to get the dreams accomplished. He may have had to move mountains and turn some bad things around for good.

When Joseph was in his upper 30s and he finally met his brothers again who had sold him into slavery, he said to them, "You meant it for harm but God has meant this for good." There had been a turn around. This is true in many of our lives. He may have had to turn some bad things for good. Don't let the passage of time rob you of God's promise. In other words, don't abort. Don't let the passage of time quench your faith because dream miracles happen over time.

It was 20 years ago that I began to study the apostolic and the prophetic at a different level. It was also then that I began to study the Ekklesia. At that time I really only knew that *Ekklesia* was the word for *church*. But God began to train and fine-tune me, shifting my focus toward learning about a true New Testament Church. One that reigns with Him affecting culture and natural government. I and others began to decree that a Third Great Awakening is going to happen in America and the world, the greatest move of God in church history.

The corporate decrees of a remnant throughout America began about 20 years ago. We began to hear prophets prophesying the Third Great Awakening and great revival is coming. Although we didn't see anything, we began to decree it. While there are those who still try to say satan has aborted it, we must understand satan always works on the basis of appearance and logic. God never does. He works on the basis of His Word and what He tells us if we will believe it.

While it may appear to some like nothing's happening, we have to understand and pursue what God is saying regardless of what we see. This is why it is vital to understand how miracles sometimes work. God has been moving in ways we couldn't see.

Like the days of Joseph, our times are converging prophetically into a "divine suddenly," and a door to the palace is opening so that the dream God gave years ago can now be accomplished. This is a season when you live resourced by the dream. God has not forgotten His promises to us, and He is watching over His Word to perform it.

Prayer

Lord, thank You that You are outside of time. We pray for Your Spirit to strengthen us afresh today. Fill us with new grace to continue to believe even when we cannot see the breakthrough coming. We believe You.

52

LITERAL PENTECOST

We decree power from Heaven is anointing us to see signs, wonders, miracles, and great harvest.

There are three literal Pentecosts that are important to understand in order to discern our times. Pentecost occurs every year and has been celebrated ever since the Exodus. They are feasts of remembrance and thanksgiving that commemorate what occurred at the first Pentecost.

The first literal Pentecost took place 50 days after the first Passover. Moses led God's people to Mount Sinai, and they camped around the mountain as Moses climbed up it to talk with God. During his time with the Lord, Moses was given God's Word, God's laws, and the Ten Commandments, and the Torah (the first five books of the Bible) began to be downloaded.

The Israelites celebrated this with a feast called Shavuot (or Feast of Firstfruits), which the Greeks called Pentecost. They celebrated God giving them harvest by bringing Him a firstfruits offering, or the first part of their harvest. Shavuot also celebrated God revealing His Word, laws, and commandments to them.

The second literal Pentecost took place in Acts 2, 50 days after Jesus became our Passover Lamb on the Cross, when Holy Spirit was poured out on the 120 who had gathered in the upper room. He came to live in believers and to fill them with power from on high so they could be Christ's witnesses. He came to anoint them with a yoke-destroying anointing, to activate supernatural gifts, and to bear His supernatural fruit. He also came to birth Christ's Church, Christ's

Kingdom, and to establish apostles, prophets, pastors, teachers, and evangelists to equip the saints to do Christ's ministry.

Holy Spirit actually came. It wasn't just a celebration of ancient history. Power from Heaven was poured out and signs, wonders, miracles, and great harvest took place. The second literal Pentecost was magnificently "more" than the other Pentecosts of thanksgiving and remembrance over the past centuries. It was far more, as Holy Spirit actually came, and they were filled with His presence and power.

Holy Spirit is saying to the Church today that we are now moving into a third literal Pentecost, far greater than Acts 2, with some new aspects added. This third Pentecost is activating the revelation of God's Word to, and through, His people in deeper ways. We will clearly see the plans and strategies that He will open to us in His Word. This new-era Pentecost will activate harvest, blessings, and power from Heaven. It is one that deploys the Ekklesia to function in higher authority and, merged with Angel Armies under Holy Spirit supervision, to disciple nations. This new-era Pentecost is surging in awesome glory and will overcome the kingdom of darkness, withering the roots and the fruit of hell with overwhelming power from Heaven. Please understand that this is not a one-time event but a continuous outpouring.

PRAYER

Holy Spirit, come again. Pour Yourself out on us today! Fill us again and again. We welcome Your glory movement.

53

ANGELS OF DELIVERANCE

We decree Holy Spirit and His angels are delivering us from confinement.

The Angel Armies are now being added in new ways, and at new levels, in this third literal Pentecost. The previous Pentecosts described angelic assistance, but now it will be far greater. Division after division of God's hosts, which have been reserved for our times, are being deployed with us. They partner to assist Christ's Kingdom government to break up, break out, break through, pass over, and possess, just as they helped the Israelites break out of Egypt, pass over, and possess their promise. And, just as they helped the people of God in the book of Acts break out of religious and government bondage, so they, too, will help us.

A host of people left Egypt with Moses, but so did the heavenly hosts that were assisting His people. It is both the people *and* the angels, and that's why it's worded this way. It's why the Scripture in Exodus 12:41 (ESV) doesn't just say the people of God left Egypt. It says, "*...all the hosts of the Lord went out from the land of Egypt.*" When you think about it, why would the Angel Armies stay? What would be the purpose?

The angels had been assisting and protecting God's people and helping Lord Sabaoth, the Lord of Angel Armies, release plagues so

His people could be free. The angels of the Lord, who were assisting the Israelites to take great wealth out of Egypt, were no longer needed in Egypt. Their assignment had been to assist God's people to break out of 430 years of bondage. Now, God has led the people out of that bondage, and the angelic hosts serving that God-ordained purpose left as well.

The Angel Armies went along with the people to protect them, to help with provisions, and to one day in the future help Almighty God break them into new lands of promise. This would begin with an amazing breakthrough at Jericho, where the walls were so thick, horse-drawn chariots could ride and patrol on top of them. Those walls were busted, shattered, and broken up by God's breakthrough angels, and God's people entered supernatural breakthrough.

> The people of Israel had lived in Egypt for 430 years. In fact, it was on the last day of the 430th year that all the Lord's forces left the land (Exodus 12:40-41 NLT).

Please note the wording—*all* the forces of the Lord left the land.

In the book of Acts, when Pentecost was fully come, Holy Spirit came to baptize God's people with power from on high. He also brought Angel Armies with Him. They are seen as tongues of fire hovering over the 120 gathered in the upper room. Angels often appear in God's Word as flames of fire, as I wrote in my first book, *Angel Armies*. They came to assist the Kingdom of Heaven to break out and to assist the apostles and the prophets in the first Ekklesia in breaking open a move of God on earth, helping to expand the newly born Kingdom of Jesus Christ.

The angels accomplished this through Holy Spirit empowerment and guidance. Now, the promise of the Lord is that it's time for another literal Pentecost. Holy Spirit is coming to pour out power from Heaven. He's coming to pour out an anointing to prevail. Just as the precedent reveals in the previous Pentecosts, He is coming with the hosts of Heaven, bringing Angel Armies with Him in far greater measure.

PRAYER

Lord of Hosts, we welcome You and the angelic army of Heaven to come. May a move of God break open on earth now, bringing Heaven to earth.

54
THE EKKLESIA

We decree Your church will prevail. The gates of hell will not prevail.

I have studied the subject of the Ekklesia for years, but about a week after Holy Spirit awakened me at Christian International in 2017, He began giving me fresh insight about the Ekklesias that He is now raising up. *Ekklesia* is the term Christ used for what He would build on earth. Here's a brief summary:

> And I also say to you that you are Peter, and on this rock I will build My church, and the gates of Hades shall not prevail against it. And I will give you the keys of the kingdom of heaven, and whatever you bind on earth will be bound in heaven, and whatever you loose on earth will be loosed in heaven (Matthew 16:18-19 NKJV).

The word *church* in this passage is the Greek word *ekklesia*. Amazingly, it's not a religious word. You would think if anyone would use a religious word to describe what He is building on earth, it would be Jesus, but He doesn't do that. He didn't say, "I am going to build My temple or synagogue." He said Ekklesia, which is a government word, used to define a ruling body like a parliament or congress. Jesus said, "I will build My congress on earth."

Ekklesia is a governing body that establishes rule in a territory. The Ekklesia in Christ's day was a ruling body that voted on and decided all laws for a region by an upraised hand. The Ekklesia was called out to do governing. The Ekklesia voted on and decided who the judges of a territory or nation would be. The Supreme Court in Christ's day, which was called the Areopagus, was chosen by the Ekklesia. Jesus most certainly knew that.

The Ekklesia sets the societal codes of conduct for a region. It has dominion. Wow. Jesus is restating the Dominion Mandate in Matthew 16. That's the word Jesus uses that is translated *church* in the New Testament. Every time you see the word *church* in the New Testament it is *ekklesia*, a governing body.

Holy Spirit began to speak to me about Christ building His Ekklesias and about the keys to those Ekklesias functioning properly. One afternoon, as I was praying and meditating this through, Holy Spirit spoke to me, and I will never forget it because it was so clear. He said, "The baptism of the Holy Spirit and the gift of speaking in other tongues is about building Christ's Ekklesias." That had my attention. He said, "It's about empowering My Ekklesias. It's about their governing intercession."

Holy Spirit began to show me the Dominion Mandate, the Ekklesia, government intercession, and praying in the Spirit as a transformative plan He uses to extend Christ's Kingdom in a region, to establish His principles, to reap His harvest, and establish His rule. I began to see that for Ekklesias to function properly on earth, it is going to take praying in the Spirit—because Holy Spirit said it's governing intercession. In Spirit language, Holy Spirit empowers and enforces, often with Angel Armies because they speak that language.

We need to allow Him to pray prayers of governing intercession. It's an advantage, He says. It's a tremendous advantage. He knows plenty that we don't know, such as timing and the positioning of Angel Armies and big-picture strategies. Let Him pray, engage, and decree, using our Spirit language.

PRAYER

Holy Spirit, pray through us today so that Your will would be done and Your angels released on earth. Build Your Ekklesia.

55

The Supernatural Enforcers

We decree we are partnering with Holy Spirit and His releasing of the mighty ones. We welcome it.

We must understand there are times when we need supernatural help. We're in one of those times now. We cannot be a true Ekklesia without supernatural power. I believe this is happening at greater levels because we now have functioning Ekklesias all over this nation and in many other nations. We have prayed and decreed millions of promises based on God's Word and His will for us.

We have learned to decree a word so it's established. We have learned to pray God's Word, declare our faith, and not back down from it. We know that no Word of God is void of power. We know that Angel Armies assist based on God's declared Word. We have also learned that words of unbelief hinder the function of angels. Idle words, idle angels. Words of unbelief can actually even anger them and stifle their work.

Holy Spirit is showing us He is releasing powerful angels to enforce the Ekklesias' verdicts rendered in the King's Name. Supernatural enforcers have been sent in greater numbers than ever before.

What a supernatural time we have moved into. Holy Spirit is now leading the plan of the Godhead for a supernatural, transitional, reformational era to begin. He has now released a host of mighty angels to enforce the verdicts of the King's Ekklesias against hell's kingdom, its princes, leadership, and their surrogate human allies in the earth realm. The King has determined His Ekklesia is going to win. It's going to prevail.

God has used this precedent from the beginning. It's a precedent seen throughout Scripture. Angels are assisting us in enforcing prayers to open nations. They are enforcing verdicts and binding evil. They are enforcing the Ekklesias' decrees to loose nations, culture, and government from demon rule. They are enforcing decrees of change and they are enforcing revival decrees. They are enforcing plans for stunning victories, breakthroughs, and Godhead surprises. Paraphrasing, King Jesus said in His definition, "My Ekklesia will rule and reign with Me in My Name. They will open doors. They'll close doors. I will give them the keys to do it. They have the keys to the Kingdom. My Ekklesia will voice My will in My Name. My entire Kingdom, all of Heaven will back them."

We have moved into a time when, supernaturally, He is going to prove it. He always does what He says. We have moved into supernatural times, and we are going to receive big wins. He has given us a verdict: "You win. Declare what I say and you will win, you will rule, and you will break through."

The supernatural enforcers have arrived and are here to assist the declared promises of God. In the Name of Jesus, we will prevail and we will win!

PRAYER

Lord Jesus, You always do what You say You will do. You never lie. Release Your supernatural enforcers now to do what only You can do.

56

Step Into the Arena

We decree that what our King says will be done.

We are called to declare the truth, and our King says, "If you will declare the truth, that is what will be done. It will produce after its kind. It will prevail." The majority of the Church has embraced the myths and distortions of demon doctrine. That twisted truth told us to stay out of government, when all along God wanted us to stay involved.

When God's people stand for biblical principles, it produces righteousness that exalts a nation. Suppressing those principles through silent surrender results in foolishness. It darkens hearts and minds and causes chaos. Who could deny that's happening today? Suppression leaves a void and empowers fools, allowing demons to rule. It hands authority over to demons.

We are in desperate need today for true disciples of Christ to arise and disciple this nation, to speak the Word of God no matter what into every level of society. It is a lie to say it's not God's plan that we get involved in social, political, or governmental issues or law. It's been His plan since day one, and it was still His plan when Jesus rose from the dead saying, "Go make disciples of all nations." It's a primary purpose of His Church, and millions are damned because the Church has not done it.

"I am giving you authority." What a statement! "Go make a stand for what I said." It is high time that we do it. The coming generation is perishing before our eyes because they lack God's perspective of reality. Listen to them—they make no sense. Listen to government—it makes no sense. I mean, how many times have I almost thrown something at my television over this nonsense? That is the definition of foolishness. It's time for us to fulfill the mandate. It's time for the sons and daughters of God to step up, make a stand, and stop the politically correct compromise. It's time to plant the Word of God into every level of society and let the chips fall wherever they fall. It doesn't make any difference what they call us. It makes all the difference to me what God calls us.

The Dominion Mandate is a message of truth that must be restored to the body of Christ. While the whole world may not see it, the remnant will see it. This means that if you are a son or a daughter of God, He has restored His original intent for you and you are to enforce it. It could be through assisting someone else, raising your voice, making a stand somewhere, or through financial means. It's time for us to embrace the responsibility. It's time to butt heads with those who say, "Be quiet." No, I will not be quiet. I am God's son. I am God's daughter. I am here to declare what He says.

We are not just commissioned to disciple as many people as we possibly can; we are also called to disciple their governance. God says we are to set the atmosphere and the parameters for good societal living. It's not either, it's both. We are to teach them what Christ says, not our ideas or opinions. We are not to give them the balanced perspective of Buddha, Mohammad, or Confucius. To disciple, we must declare what God says and engage in governing issues and laws accordingly. We are planting God's Kingdom, setting it, laying its foundation, and never backing off.

PRAYER

King Jesus, we will say what You say. Give us boldness to step into the arena and disciple nations, taking our stand as Your strong and believing Ekklesia.

57

STRATEGIES OF THE SPIRIT

We decree we are entering the season of increased dunamis—entering the season of increased Kingdom energy. We are entering the season of Kingdom fireworks.

To accurately interpret the era in which he lived, Daniel received insight and understanding through various means. He would study and pray through the meaning behind dreams, visions, and prophetic words. Daniel could solve complex mysteries, which speaks to things that are hidden from the obvious, and he also interpreted angelic visitations and what those angels communicated to him.

Daniel accomplished all these things through Holy Spirit inspiration. Jesus said that Holy Spirit is our Helper and Teacher in John 14:26. One way in which Holy Spirit assists us is through angels. Hebrews 1:14 (KJV) says, "*Are they not all ministering spirits, sent forth to minister for them who shall be heirs of salvation?*" Angels and their workings occur throughout the book of Daniel. Daniel said that he saw mighty princes assisting God's people. In Daniel 7:10, he saw ten thousand times ten thousand (one hundred million) angels assisting Father God around the throne of Heaven.

We need to understand this, as it is instructive for our times. Thousands of angels had assisted the people of God in getting out of Babylonian captivity. It was not just the archangels, Michael and Gabriel, but also the Angel Armies they commanded who battled against the Prince of Persia—a demon prince—and his demon armies. They were battling in the spirit realm to open up some doors for Daniel in the natural realm. This mighty division of angels is here today to assist the heirs and the Ekklesia of Christ Jesus. If God chose to use this division of angels, how much more important is it for us to be assisted by them as well. They are here and will hearken to the voice of our decrees made in the Name of King Jesus.

This angel division has not stopped working; it worked with God in Heaven, and it works with us on earth. There are simply times when, in spiritual conflict on earth, we must have the assistance of this mighty cavalry coming to our aid. It is available and one of the greatest benefits Holy Spirit is bringing to assist the glorious Ekklesia Jesus is building. This division has not died. There are no angel graveyards. They have not been retired. They are available as Holy Spirit leads, and we need to start getting the understanding of that spiritual dimension into our thinking.

I believe we are now moving into an era when Angel Armies, activated by Holy Spirit, will bring to pass the decrees of faith of the Ekklesia, helping bring to pass the strategies of Holy Spirit on earth. The greatest decade ever planned by Holy Spirit is now unfolding before us and we're going to see more angel activity and more divisions of angels released to assist than in any other decade in all of church or world history.

The Ekklesia of King Jesus will experience the backing of Heaven's cavalry. They are here to assist God's heirs—the joint heirs with Christ—and they are going to do exactly that. Hell will find itself facing an awesome remnant warrior church army, and it will also find itself facing the chariots of fire that Heaven is activating on earth. And, just as Elisha's servant saw, there are more of Heaven's elite warriors with us than those that are against us.

PRAYER

Holy Spirit, thank You that even now Your angels are at work on behalf of Your people. Thank You for the backing of Heaven's army. Infuse us with new zeal today to see Your Kingdom come and Your will be done.

58

THE GLORY OF THE KING

We declare it's time for a glory surge!

While it is impossible for God to become more glorious than He already is, it is possible for Him to reveal more of that glory to us than He has ever revealed before. We are going to see the fullness of His glory in Heaven, but we can see even more of His glory—His manifest presence, splendor, and power, the essence of who He is—now on earth. This is promised to us throughout the Scriptures. We are entering times when the days we have prophesied, longed for, and prayed for are going to be fulfilled.

To properly understand this word, we must understand that there is no Scripture that ever says the glory of the Lord will decrease on earth. It speaks of increase every time. Yes, darkness increases on earth, but when it does, God's glory increases upon His people. Darkness, even gross darkness, is prophesied and the Church has done a great job of declaring that. In fact, the Church has had no problem believing and stating it's going to get worse and worse. The implication is Jesus is going to have to come and save us. That's not where my focus is because as that happens, a far more exceeding weight of glory comes upon God's people. That's not been emphasized. Surges of Christ's glory are promised as darkness thickens. The weightiness of who He is will increase.

Glory is often described in Hebrew and Greek as the weight of something or someone. Weight is the total of who you are when you present yourself, the essence of your being. Glory will grow heavier and heavier, overwhelming darkness with light, overwhelming hell's tactics with greater glory. Those who say Christ's glory will diminish on an exasperated Church should consider 2 Corinthians 3:18 where Paul said it's from glory to glory to glory. It increases as by the Spirit of the Lord. Greater glory is going to be seen on the New Testament Church like it has never been seen before. It does not diminish.

The prophet Isaiah prophesies glory to God's people in Isaiah 60. Hear it as a fresh *rhema* word of the Lord. Hear it as one who is destined to flow in a more exceeding weight of glory because that is your destiny.

> Arise, shine; for thy light is come, and the glory of the Lord is risen upon thee. For, behold, the darkness shall cover the earth, and gross darkness the people: but the Lord shall arise upon thee, and his glory shall be seen upon thee (Isaiah 60:1-2 KJV).

This is the word of the Lord for this new era. It is a word to believers in Christ who have served Him through some very dark times. He is saying it's time for another surge of My glory and it's going to change the seasons. Christ will now present His presence at greater and greater levels, heavier and heavier, and it's going to change history.

Paraphrased, Isaiah says, "Get out of bed. Wake up. Rise from depression. Rise from discouragement. Quit lying down under circumstances that have kept you bound and rise above them in the greater glory. Get up and get going. Put your face toward the sunlight of God's glory and begin to move into it. His glory will be seen upon you. His glorious presence will break over you. Arise and shine, your light has come and the glory of the Lord has risen upon you." *It is time for a glory surge.*

PRAYER

Holy Spirit, we welcome the weight of Your presence to increase and grow among us. We welcome it. We welcome Your presence, Lord, at levels the world has never seen before. We welcome You, God of Glory.

59

A Supernatural Era

We decree Your Ekklesia is arising and we are seeing a reformational, supernatural awakening explode in this "now" season.

Holy Spirit is saying:

> "Follow Me into a supernatural era. One that will be dramatically different, erupting in Godhead activity. One that sees God's manifest presence filling the earth realm more and more. One that sees what is impossible to man made possible. One that is filled with outpourings. One that activates the fires of the greatest reformation in history. One that starts an era of massive soul harvest. One that sees the amazing transitional precedence of Christ's first coming to earth, seen in our times. One that sees the assistance of seraphs and Angel Armies, helping us to accomplish strategies, plans, and operations that have been secret and are now being revealed that God has purposed for our times. Follow Me into an era that sees the King's Kingdom accelerate in the earth realm."

To see the reformation that we must see in the world is going to take the supernatural. It's going to take miracles to get it done. It's going to take what's impossible to us being done by the God who begins to manifest His presence in greater measure.

The Holy Spirit says it has begun!

I believe this is a focus of Holy Spirit right now in this era. He is going to be using the heirs, the Ekklesias, and powerful Angel Armies to accelerate this prophetic word. It has to happen sometime because there is not a word that God speaks that cannot be accomplished. It's time for this amazing prophetic word to begin, as God's presence is rising in the earth realm in great measure. It will continue to rise in greater manifestations, and that can happen even in the midst of gross darkness, as Isaiah 60:2 (my paraphrase) states, *"In the midst of gross darkness, His glory arises."*

I believe in this era, the supernatural signs will include those that were seen in the Exodus and at the temple dedication, when the visible cloud of God's presence and the fire of God were seen. I don't know how or where that's going to take place, but it has happened in the past and it's part of the precedent. Somehow, the manifest presence of the Lord is going to be clearly seen. His glory will manifest more and more, and seraphs will assist its happening; it's some of what they do.

The world can attempt to run from God. It can try to bury His presence, but Holy Spirit promises the earth will be filled with an awareness of the glory of the Lord, of who He is. An increasing weight of that glory presence will be seen upon the Ekklesias, drawing people from everywhere.

Heaven's Angel Armies, who were protecting everything surrounding the birth of Jesus, briefly paused that night in what they were doing and began to give glory to God, singing praises to Him. They could be seen in the skies doing this, and as they began to sing, the glory of the Lord lit up the earth as a mighty angel declared, *"Glory to God in the highest, and on earth peace, goodwill toward men!"* (Luke 2:14 NKJV).

Another announcement is being made in our times, and I believe Michael and Gabriel, along with other angels, are assisting with this one too. The King is coming in greater manifest glory and power. A new era of supernatural reformation begins and Christ's Kingdom will accelerate forward, growing and expanding exponentially, and hell's kingdom will not stop it.

PRAYER

Lord Jesus, we cry out for Your glory to come and fill the earth! In the midst of darkness, You, the Light of the World, come and reveal to us who You are.

60
THE COMING HARVEST

We decree the power of the Holy Spirit is being released and hell cannot stop it.

The Lord gave me the following word that I declared at a recent Prophetic Summit:

> "My seraphs will proclaim messages from the Godhead. Do not be surprised by this. Expect this. They will assist the bringing to pass of prophetic words that are now at full term. There are some at full term. They will battle the delay tactics of the forever loser. Supernatural reformation will amp up and roll through the earth as Heaven's King and His Kingdom take center stage. He will not be upstaged by fools. His church will prevail. The earth will shake. Everything that can be shaken will. His Kingdom will not. You will not.
>
> "You will hear the sound of evangelists rising on university campuses. They are rising with great boldness, says the Lord, to preach the Gospel of the Kingdom. They disdain compromise. Passionate ones will rise and I will anoint them, confirming My Word on lawns, walkways, dormitories, and meeting halls with signs, wonders, and with miracles. Great visible miracles and healings will be seen that will be viral through their social media.
>
> "For the young ones have My heart. They are part of My harvest. I will Father them. They will not be fatherless. I will redeem them and re-dream them. I will place the breaker anointing upon

young men and women, and they will walk the campus declaring, 'This is the way. Walk in it. This is the way. Walk in it. This is the way. Walk in it.'

"The love draw of My presence will reach to them in waves of grace. I will reach into the hearts of those now bound, lost, deceived, and drifted with aimless mindsets. I will draw them to their purpose, calling to the deepest parts of their being concerning dreams I have put in them before they were ever born. I will call them to destiny that has been buried by lies, buried by cultural confusion and doctrines of demons. But they will run with Me as freedom heirs, champions of My cause.

"Prophets will rise to walk the campuses as I pour out My Spirit upon them and you will hear prophetic words come from college campuses from the young prophets who are on fire with My presence. They will proclaim My Word to student bodies, to wicked ideologies, to perversion. My young champions will prophesy to evil government against the intrusion of Baal. They will not back down. I said I would pour out My Spirit upon them. I meant it. Waves of fresh Pentecost fire will blaze in them and through their voice. For now begins the supernatural, transitional, reformational new era the Godhead has planned."

Prayer

Lord, thank You that Your supernatural enforcers are here to help us and aid us in bringing the Kingdom of Heaven to earth. Stir the heart of Your Ekklesia today to move forward and not delay.

61

The Strategy of Heaven

We decree the supernatural enforcers will enforce Your Word in our lives.

Holy Spirit continued with the prophetic word...

"My strategies are being implemented through the earth realm. Ekklesia strongholds have been established. Their territories have been sown with My seeds of transition. The remnant has been prepared to stand and they are pawing the earth as war horses, anticipating battle. The apostles have received initial assignments. Coals of awakening and reformation are now raging fires within them. My prophets have been anointed with eye salve. Their seers will see more clearly. I am giving them penetrating vision to spirit realms. Uncompromising pastors, evangelists, teachers are receiving the spirit of wisdom, revelation, and enlightenment as a synergizing unity of the King's remnant leaders rises to lead with great boldness. Time and places are now connecting to a supernatural moment.

"Outpouring after outpouring after outpouring will rain down on the saints of the Most High as promised will come. They are not seasonal rains. They are in every season. You will surely shift from declarations of 'this will be' and 'this is that.' This is that which our Father spoke. This is that spoken by our King. This is that spoken by Lord Sabaoth, Commander of Angel Armies. This is that spoken by the same Spirit that raised Christ from the dead. This is that spoken by our apostles and our prophets. This is that decreed and stood for by a holy remnant warrior band. This is that which Kingdom intercessors have fought for.

"The world will see in this supernatural, transitional, reformational era that I am the God of yesterday. I am the God of the eternal future, and I am God of the now. My Ekklesia will demonstrate I am the now God. My Word is alive and true now. Victory is now, says the Lord. Deliverance is now, says the Lord. Healings and miracles are now. Freedom is now. Revival is now. Harvest is now.

"Align your heart, Ekklesia, align your words of power, remnant army. Declare this is that which our God has promised. Declare now, now. Know that time and places are connecting to My promise. Know, says the Lord, that I have opened the angel gate of Heaven for you. Angels are descending and they are ascending as needed. Angel Armies are now deployed. They are surrounding My Ekklesia strongholds all over this nation and world.

"Government angels assisting the authority decrees of My Ekklesia have been sent. Awakening and reformation angels, the reapers, have been sent. Breakthrough angels shouting, 'Break up, break out, and break through,' have been sent. Evangelism and harvest angels have been sent.

"Division after division has been sent and I have now sent the mighty ones of the seraphim order from the throne room to assist you. Michael and Gabriel have been commissioned as in the days of Daniel during that time of transition into promise. What they and their armies did then, they will do now. And as in the skies of Bethlehem, they will prepare the way for the glory of the Lord to shine round about the earth realm in transitional times. In transitional times the glory will rise in transformation ways. Yes, the whole earth will become aware of the glory of the Lord."

PRAYER

King Jesus, Your word is coming to pass here and now. May the world see and know Your glory. Kingdom of Heaven, come!

62

THE AGGRESSIVE REMNANT

We decree that the Ekklesia is becoming stronger and stronger!

We have to stay focused on what God says. We have to stay focused on what Holy Spirit is saying rather than what we see going on all around us, because His Word is going to prevail.

Many years ago when Holy Spirit began to teach me about Angel Armies, I was out at a lake not far from The Oasis. I had been praying most of that week, seeking the Lord, and He stopped me in my tracks. I thought He actually spoke this word out loud. I don't think it was, but it was that bold. He said to me: "The greatest days in church history are not in your past; they are in your present, and they are in your future."

I believe we are now entering a far greater weight of glory than has ever been seen. I know that's a big statement but I believe it. A heavier, demonstrably real, manifest presence of God is about to be seen. His presence is going to enable His Ekklesia to win victory after victory after victory. We are in that season now. There's an aggressive nature coming into the remnant as the harvest of the end of the age is now being pursued and is about to be reaped. There's a Kingdom surge that is about to take place with this movement. It's like the body of Christ now understands the urgency as Holy Spirit has turned up the intensity—and the promise of 2 Corinthians 3:18 is beginning to accelerate. We are beginning the glory journey. From glory to glory to glory.

Heavier and heavier. This promise must mean the Church will become stronger and stronger and stronger not weaker and weaker.

Christ is not coming for a weak Church! Clearly, hell has never experienced anything like it's about to experience and the Church has not done some of what it is about to do. I believe the outpouring of the end of the age that has been prophesied, prayed over, and confessed for years is now beginning and it's going to roll through America and around this world.

We need to see a prophetic picture of our times in Acts 2. It's a word that is descriptive of the new era and begins to prophesy to us what is about to take place. As we recall the beginning of the New Testament Church, we can declare that truly the greatest days in church history are not in our past, but in our present and in our future! The Holy Spirit will do it again.

> And when the day of Pentecost was fully come, they were all with one accord in one place. And suddenly there came a sound from heaven as of a rushing mighty wind, and it filled all the house where they were sitting. And there appeared unto them cloven tongues like as of fire, and it sat upon each of them. And they were all filled with the Holy Ghost, and began to speak with other tongues, as the Spirit gave them utterance (Acts 2:1-4 KJV).

PRAYER

Holy Spirit, as You fell on those at Pentecost, fall on us again. Let the weight of Your glory overwhelm us. And may those around us behold what the power of Your Spirit can do!

63
REVIVAL WINDS

We decree new breath is entering God's people and a great army is rising.

In Ezekiel 37, we see a prophetic vision and hear a prophetic word. A "new breath" is entering God's people and resurrection life will cause them to come together and stand as a great army. As I pondered this important prophetic vision, I began to hear, in the spirit realm, the sound of a rushing mighty wind. I heard it for hours; it was the sound of a rumbling, from deep within.

I've hunted for elk high in the Rocky Mountains and, on some occasions, I've witnessed the treetops bending and rustling as the wind picked up. I've heard the thundering begin to vibrate deep in the forest—a roaring type of sound, off in the distance, that became louder and louder as it approached. That's comparable to what I began to see and hear in the spirit realm as I meditated on this passage.

On the day of Pentecost in Acts 2, a small remnant of 120 believers sat in an upper room in Jerusalem. They must have heard a similar type of sound from Heaven as Holy Spirit came as a rushing mighty wind, filling the house in which they had gathered. Life burst forth and transformation came as God's breath blew upon them and resurrection surged into a hopeless, fearful body of people. Disciples, buried by difficult situations and loss, came alive. Widows, orphans, and the poor, who had been entombed in societal grief and governmental domination by the Roman Empire, were revived.

As I heard the rushing mighty wind, I discerned it was coming from Heaven upon the remnant warriors who have been making their stand for Christ. I thought of the song "Revival" by Robin Mark:

> I can hear that thunder in the distance
> Like a train at the edge of town
> I can feel the brooding of Your Spirit
> Lay your burdens down, lay your burdens down.

I began to picture sails, as on a ship, rising into Holy Spirit winds. A knowing in my spirit came—winds were going to blow the Church from the doldrums into fresh waters and new ports of blessing. Holy Spirit was bringing fresh breath to "life" His body; it would no longer be a disconnected skeleton. The graves would be opened and the Church would come to life.

There is a cure for deadness. It's called "resurrection," and our King has it mastered. I don't hear funeral dirges, as some are proclaiming. I'm not hearing the bugle playing taps. I hear the sound of reveille. I hear resurrection life being breathed from the throne room. Like Elijah, I hear the sound of an abundance of rain. A fresh outpouring of God's Holy Spirit is on the move. A trans-generational anointing is available and the most alive body of people in history is emerging. They will possess the mountains of society, and hell will not overcome them.

Our King, along with Holy Spirit and His strategies, assisted by millions of angels, is working now to breathe life into the true Church. It is accelerating into a spectacular movement confirmed by signs, wonders, miracles, healings, breakthrough, and harvest. A billion-soul revival is coming; and a Kingdom move of God, greater than most have ever thought possible, has begun.

Prayer

Lord Jesus, we pray for Your Ekklesia to receive the breath of Your Spirit. Breathe life into us again so that we may run full speed ahead, empowered by the wind of Your presence.

64

HEALING WELLS

We decree healings and miracles are accelerating, in Jesus' Name.

The angel divisions of healings and miracles are activating for our times. At the beginning of 2013, I began to have a recurring vision. In the vision, I saw land oil pumps, like you see in the countryside, pumping oil. The lever on these pumps goes up and down, up and down, over and over. However, in my vision, it wasn't a lever doing the pumping—it was an angel. After seeing this vision several times, Holy Spirit spoke to me, saying, "These are angels of healings and miracles. They are pumping the old healing wells and opening new ones."

That really spoke to me because of my heritage. My father was a healing evangelist, and I have been around healing evangelists all my life. I have seen so many miraculous healings. No one could ever tell me miracles aren't real; I've seen them with my own eyes. When my brother, Dutch, and I were about 12 and 13 years old, we were the "catchers" at the altar. Part of our assignment was to clean up the cancers that were left on the floor after people were healed. We used to go to church early on Wednesday nights because people would sometimes be brought to the service in ambulances to be prayed for. We would hold open the doors and help push them in on their stretchers. That probably wouldn't even be allowed to take place today, but back then it did.

I saw so many miracles growing up, it was ingrained into me that God can do anything. I would believe that anyway, because it's in

God's Word, but it's at a different level for me because I truly saw miracles take place. At one point, when my dad was pastoring a little church of about 30 to 45 people, he and other local pastors would get together and have a summer revival. They would pray for the sick and, again, Dutch and I would be the "catchers" at the meetings.

One time we were at a small church in Hamilton, Ohio, and there were around 40 people in attendance. We had to sit on the front row because Dutch was always goofing off and Dad didn't trust us to sit anywhere else. At this particular meeting, something happened I will never forget as long as I live. A man in a wheelchair was pushed up to the front row where we were sitting. He was completely twisted up, like a pretzel. Three of the local preachers gathered around him, praying in the Spirit, and I could hear bones begin to pop, like when a chiropractor works a person. That man began to unwind in his chair and then jumped up onto his feet. He was totally healed, and I will never forget watching that take place.

The Holy Spirit is activating angels to uncap the old healing wells. We must position ourselves and be ready for what is about to take place.

Prayer

Jesus, I believe that nothing is impossible with You. Uncap the wells of the past healing movements. Open the blind eyes, strengthen lame legs, eradicate disease. Increase our faith!

65

OUR FATHER'S DNA

We decree we will be fruitful and we will multiply, exercising our dominion in Christ's Name.

Philippians 2:13 (KJV) shouts this grace-filled truth: "*For it is God which worketh in you both to will and to do of his good pleasure.*" J.B. Rotherham's translation says, "*For it is, God, who energiseth within you, both the desiring and the energising, in behalf of his good pleasure.*" God's seed in you energizes you to create God's will by decreeing His Word. His seed becomes a creative force in the heavens and the earth when decreed by those who have His DNA, His *spora* (Strong's G4701). It is His plan that when His heirs open their mouth, creative spheres will open. Power to change things and bring order out of chaos will be released. Your spirit has been seeded with the DNA and nature of the Living God.

Seed (*spora*) means "parenting seed, fertilized seed, or activated seed containing genetic markers, codes, or traits." It means "hereditary qualities and potentialities that are transmitted to offspring." A fertilized seed contains the parents' genetic markers. A parenting seed holds genetic codes and also generational markers.

The Holy Spirit conveys an incredible truth in the New Testament about being born again. The moment you received Jesus as your Lord, God sowed His Spirit and His Word into your heart and you were born again by the incorruptible seed (*spora*) of God's Word. His parenting seed was sown into you and fertilized in your spirit. It was activated, germinated, and "lifed." Qualities and potentialities from God were transmitted to you, His offspring, much like how the seed in Mary's womb was fertilized, allowing Jesus to be supernaturally born of a virgin. You were born-again—this time not through corruptible seed but by the Holy Spirit and God's incorruptible Word sown into you.

Now of course, God's seed sown into your heart produces God because it produces after its kind. It's a law of perpetuity. A God-seed produces His genetic codes in your spirit. You really are a son or daughter of God. New Testament teaching is clear, and it's affirming that the parenting seed of God is sown into you at the new birth. You have God-markers in you, literally! They are planted in the core of who you are. You are born of God.

God wants to energize His creative nature in you. You have been redeemed and restored to create with word seeds. Your words can create openings for God's purpose on earth and His will in the nations. Your words plant the heavens with divine principles and create an environment for them to exist on earth. The Dominion Mandate is not some phantom mandate that God has forgotten about. It is an eternal principle. It is expected that God's redeemed ones will rule, reign, and exercise dominion in Jesus' Name. It is Godhead approved. It has His Kingdom and Angel Armies backing it. We can seed the heavens with the Words of God, creating change and releasing His power. We can extend His rule on earth by planting the heavens with energized, activated words.

Those who are born-again ones, who have had God's seed sown into them, can now declare words that are seeds just like He did. It's part of who we are. It's part of the newborn nature God passed on. Our words spoken in faith in Christ's Name become seeds that produce after their kind. Our words in His Name are anointed to come to pass. We are to rule with them.

PRAYER

God, Your seed lives in us! Fill our mouths today to declare Your Word with fresh vigor and boldness. May our words of faith plant seeds in our homes, families, and regions that produce after their kind.

66

God-Given Rights

We decree our words will disciple nations.

In the beginning, God said *"be"* and it was. *"Trees be,"* and they were. The words produced after their kind. *"Sun be,"* and the sun was. That word produced after its kind. He planted the heavens and the earth with word seed decrees. Now, we have been restored because of Calvary, because of the Cross, to plant word seed decrees. We are to make decrees of faith based on God's Word and His will. We have been reborn to say "be." "Be" to what needs to be done, "be" to what needs to be produced. It is time for us to be who we really are. The world is crying out for the manifestation of the sons and daughters of God.

My earthly father and mother passed on genetics that can still be seen in me today. But my spirit has God's DNA in it. I am God's son—I really am! *Son* is not just some word that sounds really nice. I am here as His offspring to decree His words of life, power, and change—words that produce after their kind. Words that plant the heavens and the earth with God's Word. Word seeds that become what God says. I am here to follow the ways of my Father who has passed them on to me. It is in my spirit. It has been fertilized, germinated, and activated inside me.

It's time we use our God-given rights as heirs of Christ to decree words that seed change everywhere. Word seed decrees that disciple a nation. Word seed decrees that declare God's power, scatter darkness, and bring order out of chaos just like His Word did in the beginning. Just like Dad did. Holy Spirit hovers until He hears God's seed declared, God's Word voiced. He's hovering today over a nation and the world, waiting for the sons and daughters of God to become the voice of God on this planet and declare His Word and not back down. It's in us to do it.

If you have confessed Jesus as Lord, He has germinated His nature as a seed inside you. You really are a child of God. Part of your restored purpose is to seed the world with His words. Never speak negative words or unbelief. They are contrary to the seed of God that is in you. Reign in His name, speaking words of life and revival. We are here as His sons and His daughters to voice His Word everywhere. As mentioned previously, the greatest days in church history are not in our past—they are in our present and in our future. Say what God says.

Prayer

Lord Jesus, I repent of words that I've spoken that have not planted Your nature. Help me remember who I am—Your child—and speak accordingly. Your words in my mouth carry life!

67

Staying Focused

We decree we will not doubt in the dark what You showed us in the light. You are infusing us with joy and peace.

I recently asked the Lord what His current word was to the Church and nation. His answer was simple, yet impactful. He said, "*Stay very focused.*" The saying, "It's darkest just before dawn," certainly applies to our present times. Darkness is presenting itself in ways that are very challenging, and the body of Christ must live lives of persevering and staying focused. We cannot allow this present darkness to blind our thinking; rather, we must set ourselves to win one of the greatest battles our nation has ever presented.

When I was a student at Christ for the Nations, a guest speaker said something that I wrote on the inside cover of my Bible. That Bible is still on the shelf behind my desk to this day. The statement was, "*Never doubt in the dark what God has shown you in the light.*" I can't tell you how many times I've practiced that statement.

Through the years, I have occasionally passed through some very dark times. Most people I know who have lived for any length of time have also passed through a few dark times. There have been times when a dark thunder cloud obscured my vision and I couldn't see my way forward. In dark times, I had to learn to pause and still myself. I learned to refocus my attention and remember what God said. I would meditate and fill my mind with promises He had given. In those moments, I allowed my faith to rise up and I would trust the promise of what God had shown me in the light. In dark times, it is important to remember what God has said in order to not allow darkness to cause disillusionment.

I've remembered that simple but powerful statement so many times. Not that the days of my life have seen a majority of dark times, thankfully, but there have been a few. I've had to draw on a joy and peace that is beyond the natural realm and walk by faith, trusting what God has promised me.

King David described this faith pilgrimage in Psalm 112:4 (my paraphrase), which reads, *"The darkness attempts to overwhelm me."* But in Psalm 27:1 (KJV), he said, *"The Lord is my light and my salvation; whom shall I fear?"*

In night seasons, which are difficult, dark times, reflect upon the bigness of God. Reflect upon His goodness, graciousness, mightiness, and the awesomeness of who He is. Think about His steadfast love and His steadfast Word that never fails.

I don't pretend to know all God is doing right now, but I do know He will not allow injustice to stifle the effort of His greatest harvest. I know He is still in control and watching over His Word to perform it. He knows how to overwhelm darkness with His glorious light.

Isaiah 60:1-2 is filled with a magnificent promise:

> Arise, shine; for thy light is come, and the glory of the Lord is risen upon thee. For, behold, the darkness shall cover the earth, and gross darkness the people: but the Lord shall arise upon thee, and his glory shall be seen upon thee (Isaiah 60:1-2 KJV).

Prayer

Father, thank You that Your glory is rising now, even in the darkness. We know You are in control and You will bring Your words to pass. Our trust is in You!

68

UPROOT

We decree the Ekklesia will rise and preside in the Name of King Jesus.

We are in a time when the true Church, the Ekklesia, must stand in the face of darkness and stubborn resistance declaring the fire-filled words of Almighty God. We are in times when we must swing the sledgehammer of God's Word against evil and trust that His Word is going to bust evil to pieces.

We must proclaim the prophetic words of Holy Spirit that He has given for our times, trusting His wisdom and trusting His brilliance to produce it. We are to be a prophetic voice to the nation as Jeremiah was.

Jeremiah 1:9-10 (NLT) says, "*Then the Lord reached out and touched my mouth and said, 'Look, I have put my words in your mouth! Today I appoint you to stand up against nations and kingdoms. Some you must uproot and tear down, destroy and overthrow. Others you must build up and plant.'*"

Can there be any doubt that in our nation, we must uproot some things? Now, that's not easy. I wish it was. Sometimes it's difficult and requires bold, strong faith. There is a stubborn resistance, but it doesn't diminish our call or our authority to uproot it. Standing for what God says will uproot it. It will tear it down over time as we stand in faith and decree His promises and prophetic words.

Some things have to be torn down and destroyed. That is the job of the Ekklesia, and the Word of God says some government wickedness will have to be overthrown. This is not going to be accomplished by passive Christianity, cowards in the pulpit, or woke, in-name-only Christians in the pews. Only those who dare trust their God would embrace this kind of call. We have been promised in the light, and we will win in due season.

Our spiritual Kingdom has been given authority or oversight over nations and kingdoms. These aren't my words—these are God's words. We also hear our King say similar things in Matthew 16:19. Whatever hell's council or government brings, He anoints and calls us to overcome and forbid it.

The Message version states Jeremiah 1:10 this way:

> See what I've done? I've given you a job to do among nations and governments—a red-letter day! Your job is to pull up and tear down, take apart and demolish, and then start over, building and planting (Jeremiah 1:10 MSG).

We have a job to do. God has appointed and given us powerful authority. The Hebrew language pictures this meaning as "to preside over." We are called to preside over from a spiritual dimension, empowered by God's Word and by Holy Spirit. We are called to preside in the Name of our King and influence the nations. We are to preside over evil and evil kingdoms by declaring the words of God.

It takes work to overthrow entrenched evils and to battle demonic princes for the soul of a nation. It's not easy to be light in the darkness. Jesus said (my paraphrase), *"In this world, you're going to have tribulation, there's going to be some trouble, but stay cheerful. I've denied its right or its power over you. My true Ekklesia will conquer and prevail."* Stay focused on what the Godhead has promised. In dark times, whether in our nation, the world, or personally, remember this word—never doubt in the dark what God has shown you in the light.

Prayer

Father God, we believe and pray that Your glory is breaking the hold of evil darkness off our nation. May the glory of our King be seen in Your Ekklesia.

69
KINGDOM KEYS

We decree the anointing to prevail is being poured upon the Ekklesia.

Praying in Spirit language activates Kingdom keys that Holy Spirit gives to us in the form of gifts. We call them "gifts of the Spirit" that are given to us, the Ekklesia, so we can function properly.

A word of wisdom can be given to the Ekklesia, and something in the future is revealed.

A word of knowledge can be given. Facts are revealed. To make proper decrees, we must know the facts.

Prophecies can be given, which give us strategies from Heaven that we can decree.

The gift of supernatural faith can be activated, a faith that is available at a different level. Doubt is removed.

Discerning of spirits can activate, which helps us to know if we are dealing with demon spirits, angel spirits, or flesh.

The gift of workings of miracles can activate and is part of the function of the Ekklesia when it gathers.

Gifts of healings can be activated—spiritual, emotional, physical.

Tongues and interpretation of tongues provide revelation and enlightenment, enabling the Ekklesia to rule properly.

These are gifts, or keys, and they are not just for the individual's benefit, like the Charismatic movement taught us. The gifts do benefit us individually, but all of them are here to help the Ekklesia supernaturally function in the power of the Holy Spirit. They are keys given to assist the Ekklesia's governing intercession.

On the day of Pentecost the first church was born. We all know that; it's common knowledge to most believers. But we have to think of it not as the first *church* being born, but as the first *Ekklesia* to ever be born. The first governing body was formed and Holy Spirit filled it. What's the first thing the Ekklesia did? They began to speak heavenly Spirit authority language. "Anything is possible" language was restored. It had to have been of utmost importance and something God purposed, or Holy Spirit wouldn't have personally come to activate it.

It wasn't just about *receiving* power from on high. It was about *releasing* power from on high. Activate power with Spirit language from your spirit by faith. You declare it in your natural language, yes, but also in your Spirit language so that there is an agreement between your mind, your emotions, and your spirit.

Praying in the Spirit is one of the keys of reigning with Christ. Clearly, without the baptism of the Holy Spirit and the gift of speaking in other tongues, there would have been no Ekklesia. Without it, the book of Acts would not have happened. Ekklesias would not have been built in Galatia, Ephesus, Philippi, Thessalonica, or Rome. Without the baptism of the Holy Spirit and the reactivating of heavenly language, there would have been no miracles. There wouldn't have been any signs and wonders. There would have been no New Testament Church. Everything revolves around the Cross and born-again ones being baptized in the Holy Spirit and praying in a heavenly language as was mandated from the beginning. The Dominion Mandate was not possible without Spirit language. There is no One more important to the success of the Church in this new era than Holy Spirit.

PRAYER

Holy Spirit, we need You. Your presence is our key. We can't do anything without You. We find our purpose in You.

70
TAPED HEARTS

We decree our emotions, minds, and souls are free, in Jesus' Name.

We have moved into a new era, a season when angels are uncapping old healing wells and opening new ones, and when miracles are going to accelerate. Not all healing is physical though; there are also emotional healings and healings of the soul and the mind. My daughter, Rachel, and her husband, Mark, have adopted two children with special needs from China—Lily and Jaidin. They brought Lily home from China when she was 14 months old, shortly before Christmas.

Carol and I consider it our job to spoil the kids at Christmas, showering them with lots of presents. Of course, Lily had never opened Christmas presents before. Her older sister, Maddie, who was seven, had opened lots of them and was frantically opening them at our house on Christmas Eve. But Lily was just sitting and watching, not really knowing what to do. Maddie began picking things out around the house that we already owned to give us for Christmas. She wrapped them, using gobs of tape, and brought them to us to open.

Lily, seeing this, began to play with the tape, instead of opening presents. I was watching all of this intently. When she was done playing with the tape, she tried to set it down but of course the tape stuck to her hand. She then reached over with her other hand and grabbed the tape and tried to set it down with that hand but again the tape stuck to her hand. She did this several times, growing increasingly more frustrated to the point of tears, not being able to get rid of the tape. Seeing her frustration, I took the tape away and we taught her how to open presents. She became a pro instantly.

I woke up in the middle of the night hearing God speaking to me about accumulated grief. I had never thought about the concept of grief accumulating, but the more I thought about it the more I realized it does happen. The older you get, the more grief in life seems to accumulate. This happens, that happens, and you think you've laid it down but really it's still sticking to the soul and you need someone bigger than you to come along and take it away.

Thankfully, the promise of our great Lord Jesus is that He came to take away grief that accumulates—the divorce, the loss of a loved one, the bankruptcy, the broken relationship. These things can accumulate in our lives, but Jesus comes to unwrap our soul and set us free, healing our emotions, feelings, and minds.

Many today need to be healed in their souls. They're walking around with taped hearts that only Jesus can set free. Thankfully, these divisions of angels that assist with healings and miracles are opening the old healing wells. They are also opening new wells of healings and miracles. Angels are assisting Holy Spirit to activate the King's anointing to heal, established through the stripes on Jesus' back, at levels the world has never seen before. You will see miracles accelerate. You will see healing accelerate in the physical realm, and you will see dramatic healings of the soul.

Prayer

Jesus, today I open my heart to You. Heal what needs healed. Mend what needs mended. Restore what needs restored.

71
NO MORE DELAY

We decree no more delays to the promises of God. No more delays.

In His name, Christ's champions will now demonstrate power delegated to them at levels and in numbers never seen before. The world has never seen anything quite like what it's about to see. A fullness of time has come. Grace and glory will now be multiplied *exponentially* and will be seen and felt *experientially* as the prevailing truth of Christ is taught and declared on earth.

When it was time for God's people to leave the bondage of Egypt and shift into the land of great promise, again we see God's glory surge. His glory was presented in fire and clouds, visibly seen leading the way to promised inheritance. A shift is now decreed from the Spirit of the Lord. Holy Spirit is saying to the Church, "Leave bondage and enter inheritance promised. Step into a season of greater glory and receive promise after promise."

When it was time to shift from a nomadic, tent sanctuary to a magnificent sanctuary that was built by King Solomon, as Solomon knelt before the Lord and prayed the prayer of dedication, God's glory surged in demonstrably, visibly, tangibly real ways. God came close. His presence surged in their midst and they were overcome by the greater weight of His presence filling the sanctuary.

When it was time to shift from law to grace at Pentecost, once again we see the glory of God surge in their midst. His glory became demonstrably real. His presence was presented with fire, wind, and sounds from Heaven. The surge of His presence among them, the increased weight of who He really is, released anointing on them to be who they really were—anointed heirs, flowing in ever-increasing grace and glory. Heirs anointed to release the purposes of God on earth in His name.

The Lord is saying to His Church, "You are now entering a season when the presence of God will surge among you." His glory will fill your sanctuaries. The weight of His presence is going to overwhelm hope deferred with wave after wave of His glorious presence. "I will change things," says the Lord. "I will change you from glory to glory to glory as My Holy Spirit fills you with outpourings of power, refreshing, giftings, and anointings, to enable and release you to be who you really are—heirs of God and co-heirs with Christ with ordained destiny."

In this new era, promises are being fulfilled. You are entering a season when promises will be fully filled by the weight of God's presence that comes upon you.

The fullness anointing that is on Jesus will be revealed at greater levels. John 1:16 (NKJV) says, *"And of His fullness we have all received, and grace for grace."* Grace that increases and multiplies to fully fill. It doesn't decrease, it never has; grace only multiplies.

When Holy Spirit emphasized this to me, I spent hours walking and decreeing, "No more delays. I bind delay in Jesus' Name. I hate delay. I resist you in the Name of King Jesus. No more delays to the promises of God. No more delays by the kingdom of darkness. No more delays to you hindering spirits. No more delays. I am stepping into a new time. I'm stepping into a new season of greater glory. I refuse to allow delay to hold me." Decree that with me today.

Prayer

We cry out to You, Lord, come. Become demonstrably and experientially real in our lives. Show us the greater levels. Let the weight of Your glory come. We agree with the message of Heaven—no more delay.

72

Kingdom Mantles

We decree Kingdom mantles are being re-soaked and given to today's Ekklesia.

There is an amazing precedent for our times seen through the story of Elijah and Elisha. Elijah lived his life as a faithful prophet of the Lord, refusing to compromise. In 2 Kings 2, the time had come for Elijah to pass on and a miraculous scene unfolded. Fifty prophets were watching as Elijah and Elisha were standing alongside the Jordan River and Elijah began to take off his mantle.

A mantle refers to evident Kingdom of God authorization that is placed upon someone by the Holy Spirit to accomplish certain callings or giftings. This mantle authorizes the person to fulfill a Kingdom of God purpose. It is important to note that these are Kingdom mantles, not owned by the individual. Rather, they are ministered through that individual under Holy Spirit power.

Elijah wore a visible coat representing he was anointed to be a Kingdom of God prophet. As they stood alongside the Jordan River, he took off his mantle and began to roll it up. He stepped to the water's edge, raised up the mantle and struck the river with it. The river suddenly parted and Elijah and Elisha walked across on dry ground. This was a miraculous moment of seeing the supernatural merge into the natural realm.

When they crossed to the other side, Elijah told Elisha to ask him for anything, to which Elisha replied, "I'm asking for a double portion of the spirit that is on you. I want to function with God's mantle that's on your life flowing in a double portion of ministry anointing on mine." Elijah replied that if Elisha was with him when he left for Heaven, he could have it.

They walked a short distance and suddenly, another supernatural event took place when a fiery chariot came out of Heaven and caught Elijah away. Quite a supernatural transition, to say the least. Supernatural transitions that pass on Holy Spirit's anointing do happen and Holy Spirit has said it now begins. Holy Spirit is passing on Kingdom mantle anointings in this era. When Elijah's mantle fell, Elisha caught it, wrapping it around his shoulders in reverence and thankfulness to the Living God.

Some time later, still wearing Elijah's mantle, Elisha walked back to the Jordan River with the 50 prophets from the guild watching him intently. When Elisha got to the banks of the river, he took Elijah's mantle and struck the river, shouting, "Where is the God of Elijah?" Again, the river divided and he walked back across on dry ground. The prophets watching this exclaimed that the same spirit in Elijah now lives in Elisha. The anointing of Elijah now flowed through him. (See 2 Kings 2:1-14.)

Holy Spirit drew me to this famous passage of Scripture and said:

> "I want you to pray for My anointings on My mantles again. Emphasize mantles once worn by the heroes of faith and pray for them to be passed down within the King's Ekklesia. I gave them, I anointed them, and can anoint them again. They are like wineskins. I can pass them on. Don't leave them lying on the ground; ask and believe for them."

PRAYER

Holy Spirit, that is what we pray. We pray that Your anointing would rest on Your mantles again. We pray today that the mantles of the heroes of the faith would be passed down now.

73
A Double Portion

We decree a double portion on the King's Ekklesia.

We must activate our faith to lay hold of Kingdom mantles. Kingdom mantles are like wineskins that can be re-soaked and reused. I believe Holy Spirit is anointing mantles to wrap around His Ekklesia. The flow of anointings, ministries, and movements in past eras will flow again in this new era along with new anointings.

Holy Spirit has given us an assignment to ask and believe for the double portion. We must ask and seek with passionate faith like Elisha did. We are being prepared by Holy Spirit to strike the earth with double-portion anointed mantles. We are being called to decree against evil and evil government, knowing our decrees are backed by the power of God. Let's dare ask for Holy Spirit to wrap the anointed mantles around our shoulders to help usher in a Kingdom worldwide revival in this era.

As I thought and prayed into this revelation, I heard over and over in my heart and spirit what the prophets said, "*The spirit in Elijah now flows through Elisha.*" Obviously, this is a reference to Holy Spirit because Elijah had already gone. It meant the Holy Spirit of God who flowed through Elijah now flowed through Elisha. As I pondered that, I heard Holy Spirit make this decree, "*The flow of anointings, ministries, and movements in past eras will flow again in this new era along with new anointings.*" And then He said, "*Here's an assignment you have. Tell My people to begin to ask for the double portion. Ask for it. Believe for it. Ask for it. Ask for the double portion.*"

I began to see the magnitude of God's plan for this era. We are being prepared by Holy Spirit to strike the earth with mantles seen in ages past and with fresh new ones He is now giving. A double-portion anointing is planned.

We have been praying for fresh outpourings of power from Heaven for many years. We are praying and embracing Holy Spirit's call to decree what God says, just like Elijah and Elisha did against evil and against evil government. We have prayed for, and are embracing, Holy Spirit's call to take hold of generational anointings on His ministers, His ministries, and movements through the past ages, such as the Voice of Healing movement.

As He synergizes them all together, empowering them to function and flow again, why not ask for a double portion? May the Kingdom of Christ in this era flow in the multiple anointings of the ages and strike the earth with the Gospel of the Kingdom. Strike the nations with Christ's delivering power. Strike the powers of hell. Strike the darkness with glorious light. Strike the oppression of the bound, the bruised, the sick, the diseased, the prodigals, the lost, the hopeless. Strike and set them free.

Prayer

Father, we ask for a double portion to be poured out over Your Ekklesia. Release fresh mantles of Kingdom assignments, drenched in Your presence, so that the broken are healed and the captive set free!

74
What You Do Matters

We declare that the Ekklesia will stand for the cause of the King!

It is time for the true New Testament Church to make a stand for awakening, reformation, and the cause of Christ as never before. To see great victories, deliverance, signs, wonders, and miracles, to see revival roll through the land, to see awakening and great reformation like Martin Luther and thousands of others down through history, a stand must be made for our cause. It is not going to just happen. If it happens, some warriors are going to have to make a stand. I feel a boldness beginning to rise up in me, in my very bones. I suppose I have always been pretty bold throughout the ministry God has allowed me to do, but there's something intense starting to rise inside of me. I've never felt quite as aggressive as I feel right now. I've never before felt the intensity in the Spirit to make a stand like I do right now.

Of course, no one ever understood and represented a cause-driven life quite like Jesus Himself. His tenacious commitment has spoken to me most of my life, time and time again. All I have to do to be inspired is to take a look at the energy and focus of Jesus. No matter what was thrown His way—storms, Pharisees, religious leaders, the government rising against Him—He was not fazed. Something about the energy of King Jesus and what He is about on this earth and in His rule as King is starting to resonate in a different way inside me, and it is going to start resonating inside believers all across the land.

Jesus' mindset represents the heart of world changers and history makers down through the centuries. Some are famous, but most are not. Most are common, ordinary people who simply make a contribution to the cause, knowing that without their stand the cause will suffer. They simply do their part, even if that part seems minuscule. It may be a behind-the-scene part, but small as it may be they are willing to push forward for the cause. It is an amazing fact of history that the millions of contributed efforts in concert together made a difference. In other words, what you do matters. *How* you pray matters. *If* you pray matters. You, and what you do, are so significant. We must understand the power of one and the synergy of millions.

Edward Hale made this statement: "I am only one, but I am one. I cannot do everything, but I can do something. And I will not let what I cannot do interfere with what I can do."

Edmond Burke said, "Nobody makes a greater mistake than he who did nothing because he could only do a little bit."

Mother Teresa stated, "If you can't feed a hundred people, then feed just one."

It's the concerted effort of remnant believers united together for the cause of Christ that can change the world.

Prayer

Lord, we pray that there would come a wooing of the Holy Spirit and that those who have been sitting on the sidelines would rise up and make their stand. Thank You, Lord, for all who have made a stand for You, but let the greatest stand now be made by Your Ekklesia.

75

Right Now

We declare the Kingdom of God is rising and rising.

In our current state of the world, many Christians have thought, *What can I do? I'm not rich. I'm not famous. I don't have a lot of influence. I'm just one.* We must begin to see again the synergy and the power of millions who raise their voices together for a cause. Yes, we are a remnant, but we are a larger remnant than we've ever been before. Millions of us do speak in tongues, move in gifts of the Spirit, and are beginning to pray. We have to become, like the early Church, people who stand together with a unified purpose, calling on the Name of the Lord, and making an appeal to Heaven. We simply must understand the power of a people who are united in agreement.

Yes, we can change the world and this nation and see the reversal of evil laws. Our Kingdom coalition forces are stronger than hell's opposition. We can see righteousness that exalts a nation. We can see revival roll throughout this world. We can see the greatest harvest in all of history and, yes, our land can be healed. But it takes a people who will make a stand for God, His Word, His cause, His purpose, His Son, Holy Spirit, and the prevailing Angel Armies to help them overcome and finally do what's been prepared for us to do—rule in the midst of our enemies.

Queen Esther had this mindset. When Mordecai, Esther's uncle, told her about the new law that had been put into place, which would affect her and her people—their goods could be confiscated, their wealth could be transferred to their enemies, they could be jailed or even killed—he said to her, "Perhaps you were born for such a time as this." Mordecai was saying, in essence, "Esther, this is why you were born! This is what you were made to do. This is why you were put upon this earth." We know that Esther embraced that mindset and did what she could.

Mordecai's statement is being said by the Holy Spirit to you and me today. He is saying, "This is the time for which you were born. You were born for right now." God could have had you born anytime He wanted. He could have had you born in the dark ages, but He has you here now because He wants you here now. You were born for this time. I feel like I am born for this time.

God wanted me here for right now. I'm not here by accident. This is my time. I was born to make a difference right now. I was born to see revival and reformation. This has to become the mindset of today's Ekklesia. It must become the New Testament Church's mindset and it ought to be the remnant mindset everywhere. No more meandering around in hopelessness; it is time to get focused on our purpose.

PRAYER

King Jesus, what an amazing time to be alive. Thank You for filling Your remnant with fresh boldness and courage today, so that we may make a stand and see Your Kingdom come in every sphere of society.

76

A Kingdom Worldview

We decree the Ekklesia is taking her rightful place, to rule and reign with Christ.

Jesus Christ came teaching the reality of the Kingdom because He wanted this truth to be the worldview of His sons and daughters. If we don't understand this, Christianity does not work as originally intended, at least not to its fullest extent. The Dominion Mandate and the Great Commission to go into all the world and disciple nations will not happen without a Kingdom worldview. That's why lucifer and his powers fight the message of the Kingdom so hard. He doesn't want us reigning with Christ in this life. He doesn't want us exercising dominion. He doesn't want us to understand what Jesus originally meant. He wants us to be ignorant and passive.

Jesus did not come to start a Kingdom that would be dormant for 2,000 years. That would make no sense. He expects His Kingdom to rule and reign with Him on earth right now. Through prayer decrees and planting God's word seeds, He expects His joint heirs to keep good foundations maintained on earth so that government can be built on a solid social structure. He expects them to, in His Name, forbid some things and permit some things. He expects His influence to enter into a culture and change that culture through His born-again ones teaching exactly what He says. He expects His Church to act like it's supposed to act and to work for what His Word says must be accomplished.

The word for *kingdom* is the Greek word *basileia* meaning "royal dominion, to rule, the realm of a king, and a kingdom's reign" (Strong's G932). The English word is composed of two other words—*king* and *-dom*, a suffix meaning "domain." A *king's domain* is his kingdom. A kingdom is a government that rules a territory, an area, or a nation. The Scriptures teach emphatically that Jesus is a King, He has a Kingdom, and He rules a territory. Naturally, His rule is boundless. His domain is everywhere—in Heaven and upon the earth. He even rules hell itself because He has the keys, which represent authority.

Jesus being King of Heaven is not argued very much among Christians. But that He is King over the earth is often dispensationalized. It's put off into the future as though the earth is not yet part of His domain or jurisdiction, which is exactly wrong. To say that would limit His authority, and you can't do that because Jesus Himself said, *"All authority has been given to Me in heaven and on earth"* (Matthew 28:18 NKJV). He spoke that word in the present tense, so that must mean that He is King of Heaven and He is King of earth right now. He is sovereign over it all right now.

How does that work? It's supposed to work through His Kingdom's Church, which is His body (see Ephesians 1:23). The Church is to be Christ's ruling body on earth. Remember from Romans 8:17, we are *"heirs of God, and joint heirs with Christ."* We are identical heirs with Christ right now, and in His Name we are to rule on earth.

PRAYER

Jesus, You are the King. I pray You open the eyes of Your Church today to see and know that we are to rule and reign with You now. Let us not put off into eternity what is meant to be lived in today.

77

CHRIST'S CHURCH

We decree Christ's Ekklesia is being restored to her original purpose.

The picture of a Kingdom that grows and prospers on earth is strengthened by the word Jesus chose to refer to His Church. After three years of teaching the Kingdom, He used a political, judicial, and governmental word to introduce His Church into the earth. That astonishes a lot of people. But remember, God wants His sons and His daughters reigning with Him. We are made in His image and He is a ruler, a governor, and a King, so the nature to govern is planted into our being the day that we are born again. It's part of our spiritual DNA.

The word Jesus uses for *Church* emphatically reflects that. That word is *Ekklesia,* and it is translated "church" 113 times in the New Testament (Strong's G1577). Jesus, the disciples, and the apostles used *Ekklesia* to describe the Church. It is not a religious word. It is not even a sacred word, and in the Bible it never denotes a building or a specific place of worship. Of course, it has come to mean that today. We say, "I am going to church today," or someone may ask, "Where do you go to church?"

Technically, that is not possible because *you are the Church*. The word *Church* originally meant an assembly of those called out for a purpose. Yes, part of that purpose is worship, part of it is teaching, and part of it is discipline, but those are not the whole purpose, and place is never a factor. You can worship any place. If Christ meant to speak of a place, He would have used the word *synagogue* or *temple.*

Notice the distinction between *Ekklesia*, an assembly or group of people, and *church*—a location with a building (and probably some people in it). This is subtle, but it is a dangerous confusion that has caused most people today to hear *church* and think place, not Kingdom. Hell's definition confines the most powerful governing body on earth, the Ekklesia, to within the walls of a building on Sunday morning.

Christ never said, "I will build My synagogue or temple, and the gates of hell will not prevail against its walls." He said, *"I will build My* [Ekklesia], *and the gates of hell will not prevail against it"* (Matthew 16:18 NKJV). Knowing who Jesus is and His brilliance, we have to conclude that He did not use this word accidentally to describe His Church. It was stated on purpose, it was Godhead planned, and no other word is ever used. It's Ekklesia in all four Gospels, in Acts, in Romans, in the Epistles, in Timothy, Titus, Hebrews, and Revelation. It is never another word. We must understand the meaning of Ekklesia if we are going to understand what Jesus intended His Church to be.

PRAYER

Lord Jesus, realign our hearts and minds to be commissioned as Your Ekklesia—a called-out group, set apart to co-reign with You. Show us who You intended us to be.

78

Evangelism Angels and the Harvest

We decree evangelism angels are being dispatched now. It's harvest time!

Jesus said a sign of the end times and His coming would be angels becoming reapers. Two angels are assigned to every person at birth. Their assignment is to pull out the destiny God has planned for them. Before you were ever born, God sat down and wrote your thesis—why He created you. Your two angels are briefed on that and they work to bring it out of you. You may rebel against that destiny, but the angels are not going to stop trying until you die (see Chapter Five in *Angel Armies*).

Evangelism angels help to draw destiny out of people and, of most importance, they draw you to Christ. You must be born again. There are three phases in this division.

Phase 1: The Prodigals

Millions of prodigals are about to come home. Many of them were raised in church and they know their Bible. We need to get them home and plugged in. I am convinced some of the greatest apostles, pastors, and ministers in this new era are prodigals who are returning to the Church. I list this category first because we have to have them and because there has been a billion-soul harvest prophesied. I was in Chicago a few years ago and prophesied that the greatest exodus in history would not be the exodus of the million souls Moses led out of Egyptian bondage. Rather, it would be an exodus of a billion souls leaving worldly bondage and returning to their roots in this new era.

Phase 2: New Converts

Brand-new, born-again ones are coming in. It's harvest time and evangelism angels are assisting in the harvest of new souls coming into the Kingdom of God.

Phase 3: Evangelists

The fivefold ministry office of an evangelist will be restored and connected to apostolic hubs. This office has to function, and we need present-day "Billy Grahams" to come forth. The potential is unlimited, and what we are about to see take place in the body of Christ is incredible.

The word *evangelism* has *angel* right in the middle of it. In the Bible, angels are God's messengers, the bearers of the good news of the Gospel. The word *gospel* is the Greek word *euangelion* (which also has the word *angel* in it) and it was used in several different ways: *Euangelion* was used to announce the news of a victor, to announce the death of an adversary, to announce the birth of a son, or to announce an upcoming wedding. It was all good news.

The word used for *good news* in the New Testament is the word *gospel*. We have good news, *euangelion,* to declare and proclaim to the world.

- Good news! There has been a victory. Calvary defeated hell's plan, and Jesus has stripped the devil of his power.
- Good news! There has been death to our adversary. Jesus destroyed principalities, powers, mights, and dominions, making a show of them openly.
- Good news! A son has been born and His name is Jesus. The angel said, "*...I bring you good tidings of great joy which will be to all people. For there is born to you this day...a Savior, who is Christ the Lord* [King]" (Luke 2:10-11 NKJV).

- Good news! We are heading for a wedding. The largest wedding celebration ever will be held in Heaven at the marriage supper of the Lamb.

We are beginning to see revival outbreaks in the land that will now accelerate worldwide.

PRAYER

Lord God, send Your evangelism angels worldwide now to bring prodigals home and unlock the destinies of Your people. May revival spring up around the world as Your good news goes forth.

79

ANGELS ON ASSIGNMENT

We decree Angel Armies are on assignment.

Multiple divisions of Angel Armies are now being sent to earth to assist an emerging and strong Ekklesia of King Jesus, a Church that embraces the opportunity to reign with Him in this life (see Romans 5:17). Holy Spirit is in charge of this campaign and is now beginning times of refreshing and outpourings of anointings to empower the heirs to function in His Kingdom, as intended. We have now entered a new-era Pentecost, greater than Acts 2, when replenishing anointings, one after the other, wave after wave, will continue to energize the glorious Church, as promised. We have moved into the season when mighty surges of Holy Spirit power will invigorate Christ's Kingdom on earth. Supernatural activity that has been seen throughout the ages in certain times and seasons will accelerate in full measure. We will now see a people who represent Jesus as He truly is, doing the same works as He did.

The divisions of Angel Armies are here to assist the people of God in serving that high purpose. I believe it is why, when Holy Spirit began to reveal Angel Armies to me years ago, one of His first statements was, "I will now lead another campaign on earth for King Jesus. It will be far greater than the one I led in Acts chapter 2 to birth the New Testament Church. But this time, I will be bringing far more of the Angel Armies. The greatest days in church history are not in your past; they are in your present and in your future."

We are moving into the awesome days we've been promised. Holy Spirit is leading the way and divisions of His powerful Angel Armies are assisting us to accomplish the new campaign here on earth. There has never been anything like it before. A global outpouring of Holy Spirit on a functioning spiritual Kingdom around the world is now being poured out.

We are now moving into the greatest evangelistic era the Church has ever seen. Evangelism and harvest angels are assisting Holy Spirit and the true Ekklesia to reap the billion-soul harvest. We will now see millions of prodigals coming back to Father's House. We will see hundreds of millions of new converts. Fiery evangelists will now rise to proclaim the Gospel of the Kingdom. Many of them are from the coming generation. We are moving toward miraculous harvest.

This is the decade when the King will make His stand on earth, assisting us to break through the obstacles of hell and the strongholds of darkness as the harvest comes forth. The Ekklesia, empowered with Holy Spirit and with angelic assistance, will break through and demolish warped philosophies and doctrines of devils. In this magnificent era, barrier walls will be smashed by the decrees of the King's Ekklesia as it begins to aggressively function as He has sworn it will.

PRAYER

Jesus, come as the Breaker, the one who stands. We know obstacles will now fall and tactics of the enemy will be dismantled as Your Ekklesia takes her rightful place, empowered by Holy Spirit.

80

DEPLOYMENT

We decree the purpose and plans for this new era cannot be reversed. It is immutable.

Holy Spirit spoke to me concerning a new era decade of greater glory and a special Pentecost that has now fully come. Here is that word:

> "It is now in its moment. This year, the Ekklesia leaves its training and begins deployment. This will be a year of deployment and change for your future. The functioning Ekklesia will rise to operate in higher authority and its advance will be rapid. The world will see the deployment of Heaven's Kingdom Ekklesia and Angel Armies. This will suddenly and aggressively be revealed. Strongholds of hell will be broken and iniquitous roots will dry up under its superior power, authority, and administered justice. The withering of hell's kingdom will begin to be seen in indisputable ways. For the heirs of Kingdom authority are being seated in their regional spheres of influence and their angels, along with the divisions of angels assisting them, are aligning with the assigning. You will now see a clear merger; Heaven and earth will merge in unified oneness of purpose to escalate the King's victories, expand His Kingdom, and implement His spiritual Kingdom's government. The merger of the earth realm with the spirit realm will surge in visible function in this new Pentecost era."

Then I heard Holy Spirit say, "The purposes and plans for this era have fully come and will not be reversed. It is an immutable decree of King Jesus for His Ekklesia."

This is the era of the Kingdom of God's Ekklesia on earth, also referred to as the "glorious church era." He's returning for a glorious Church and it's going to happen sometime, so why couldn't it happen now? This is the season when the glorious Church era begins and we enter into the new boundaries that have been set. Holy Spirit says, "The purposes and the plans have fully come and they will not be reversed." It is an immutable decree of King Jesus for His true Ekklesia. This is its "prepared for" moment—the right time, the right era. Our King has sworn both His and His Kingdom's assistance, as well as angelic participation. He has seven'd Himself to rise and fulfill the prophetic word of Micah 2:13, running before His Kingdom Ekklesia, ensuring that they will break through.

The King, the Breaker Himself, will put His Ekklesia on His shoulders and run with them. Think about that. It's not about whether or not *we* can do it; it's about whether or not *He* can do it. He swears, "I'm going to do it. I'm going to bust up roadblocks, move mountains, and break you through. You're going to be who I say you are, who I have prepared you to be. You are going to do what I've said you will do. I give My oath that the gates of hell will not prevail against My Ekklesia. All the powers of hell combined will not overcome you. It's unchangeable; no compromises, mutations, or appeasing doctrines. I stake My reputation on it. It's immutable."

Prayer

Lord, we partner now with Your words: the gates of hell will not prevail against Your Ekklesia. Fill us again today with the power of Your Spirit. Come, King Jesus.

81
RE-SOAK

We decree the Kingdom of Christ in this era to flow in the multiple anointings of the ages and strike the earth with the Gospel of the Kingdom.

The King's Ekklesia today must rise and take hold of generational anointings, along with destiny mantles planned for us before we were ever born.

Dare we ask for the Kingdom mantles once worn by heroes of faith to be placed on our shoulders? Dare we ask they be soaked again in anointing and passed on to this generation? Dare we ask for a double portion? Dare we say their mantles will not lay on the ground? Place them on us!

Dare we say the wells they dug will not be stopped up? We will pump them again. Dare we say the ground they possessed, we will not give to the enemy? Dare we ask the hard thing, the hard thing in human eyes that was clearly not hard to God? Dare we embrace Holy Spirit's mantles, Kingdom mantles, declaring expectant faith?

Where is the Lord God of Elijah? It wasn't a negative question Elisha asked then and it's not one now. It was an expectant shout of an anticipated answer and God gave that answer, rolling the river back, as Elisha walked through on dry ground (see 2 Kings 2). In other words, let's see Him divide waters again. Let's see Him move supernaturally in our times.

Where is the Lord God of Peter, James, and John? Is He not the same yesterday, today, and forever? Where is the God of Abraham, Isaac, and Jacob? Where is the God of Noah? Where is the God of Gideon? Where is the God of Mordecai and Esther? Ruth or Deborah? Where is the God of David? Where He has always been—ruling and reigning over the nations from His holy throne in Heaven (Psalm 47:8).

Would someone dare pick up that warrior King mantle and take out some giants, please? Would the King's Ekklesia dare wrap a double-portion mantle around their shoulders of deliverance anointings, of taking back what the enemy has stolen, of changing and rewriting evil oppressive laws and an anointing that would see the world awakened and reformed?

Dare we ask Him to resoak those mantles that saw incredible healings and miracles that captured the attention of the world? Those Kingdom mantles can be re-soaked again and given to today's Ekklesia.

I believe Holy Spirit is mantling the Ekklesia in this era with multiple mantles. Christ's Kingdom is growing and expanding, empowered by the Holy Spirit to disciple people and nations. This synergy of the ages will empower us to see the greatest harvest of souls that's ever been, the greatest days in church history, and the greatest outpouring of signs, wonders, and miracles. We will see our great God make known who the God of this nation is and who the God of this world is. He has a plan, it's going to work, and we get to participate in it.

Prayer

Lord Jesus, Your Kingdom is coming and coming now. We believe it. Ready us, Holy Spirit, as You anoint Your Ekklesia to see the greatest harvest, the greatest days, and the greatest outpouring the world has ever seen.

82

DIVINE RESPONSIBILITY

We decree our God will not be defied. We will stand for our King!

The kingdom of hell is still trying to defy the Church. The kingdom of hell still offers an open challenge to the Church of Jesus Christ and His Kingdom.

Today, that challenge of hell is thrown in our faces. I hear it every single day. I hear the defiance come against the people of God, against our King Jesus. I hear the defiance on mainstream media, newspapers, and various media platforms: Your God can't fix this.

That defiance comes to us in the form of humanism that says, "Your God's not God; man is god himself." That is the dominant teaching now of humanist temples in the United States. That's what I call colleges—humanist temples that teach the humanist religion. Do you know that in many colleges today, the Church is labeled as the Christian Taliban? The defiance comes at us every single day in the form of immorality: "Your God's not God; sex is god. Lust is god now; serve pleasure." It comes to us in the form of idolatry: "Your God's not God, Maharaji is god. Muhammad, he's the same as Jesus. Buddha's god. Muhammad's god. Satan is god." A few years ago, some nominal churches (nominal meaning "in name only") even began putting the Quran in the back of the pew alongside the Bible, calling it Chris-lam.

We are defied every single day. It comes to us in the form of drugs. Drugs are worshiped religiously. That defiance comes to us in the form of government laws that are anti-Bible, which makes government assume the role of god, purging the culture of all Christianity. "We don't care what your God said; we say that homosexual marriage is fine. We say Roe v. Wade is fine." It comes to us in the form of activist judges who say, "Take the prayer out of schools, and by the way, don't mention Jesus. Don't mention Him at Christmastime. In fact, don't even mention Christmas. You have to call it a winter holiday. Take those Ten Commandments down off your walls." Lee Greenwood isn't even permitted to sing in some of our schools, "God Bless the USA."

Yes, the Church is defied daily by various forces of sin that say, "Your God's not God; we know who god is. Our god is the real god. Humanism is the real god. Narcissism is really what you ought to serve." Defilement comes at all levels. In 2006, it was said by our own former US President, Barack Obama, that "America is no longer a Christian nation...."[2] Where are those warriors who will stand up and say, "Oh, yes, we are! We always have been. It's our history. It's our inheritance. Our roots say differently." It's past time to make our stand. Little wonder God has been building all this up, converging the ages and synergizing all the past outpourings and saying to us, "Here they are; make your stand."

Famed theologian, physician, and Nobel Prize recipient Albert Schweitzer wrote, "Man must cease attributing his problems to his environment, and learn again to exercise his will—his personal responsibility." Responsibility is from two obvious words—*response* and *ability*. You have response-ability. You have an ability to respond. We are responsible to steward this world in accordance with the Word of God. We are responsible to serve the cause of our great God. We are responsible to disciple our nations. We are responsible to stand for our King in an aggressive manner.

PRAYER

2 J. Randy Forbes, "Obama Is Wrong When He Says We're Not a Judeo-Christian Nation," *US News and World Report,* May 7, 2009, https://www.usnews.com/opinion/articles/2009/05/07/obama-is-wrong-when-he-says-were-not-a-judeo-christian-nation.

Lord, relight the cause again in everyone who is willing to stand up for the cause of Your Kingdom. Light it, Lord, in such a way that the world will see a Kingdom rising up that will make a difference.

83

THE MEGA OUTPOURING

We decree a mega outpouring of the Holy Spirit has begun and there is no crisis in the natural realm that can stop this move of God.

I believe we are now moving into a literal new Pentecost, an incredible outpouring of Holy Spirit. This will be the largest activation in all of church history, and it is due now. Our God's prevailing anointing of favor is going to soak the people of God, the true Church, and we are going to see the greatest move of God that has ever been seen on earth.

All of the streams and all of the moves revealed from Acts 2 until now, all of them, will now function, held together and anointed to succeed by what I can only call a mega outpouring of Holy Spirit.

There is no crisis in the natural realm that can stop it. It will only backfire on hell because the anointing is going to turn things in our favor. It's not that we don't go through crises, because we do. It's not that tough times don't come against us, because they will. It's not that confinement and activities of darkness don't attack us, but we are anointed with favor. The anointing of our God and King, Holy Spirit and His Kingdom, will simply begin to cycle us from barrenness to greater productivity. Greater is He who is in us than he that is in the world (see 1 John 4:4).

This is actually the teaching of the New Testament apostles. It is most certainly what the apostle Paul taught the Philippians, writing to them from jail—a place of confinement—which was his punishment for preaching the Gospel of Jesus Christ. He shared some principles that I believe connect some of the dots for us prophetically today. Philippians 1:12 says that this will only cause a furtherance of the Gospel. Paul said his imprisonment, along with everything else that had happened to him, had resulted in some of the believers becoming bolder than they ever had been in declaring the Gospel of King Jesus. He also said concerning himself that persecution resulted in his being able to present the Gospel of the Kingdom to ethnic groups that he ordinarily would not have been able to reach, actually furthering the Gospel. Paul then said in Philippians 1:19 that this will actually turn for our deliverance.

I love this in The Message Bible: Paul states, *"They didn't shut me up; they gave me a platform!"* (Philippians 1:20 MSG).

Paul also wrote in Philippians 1:6 (MSG), while in confinement, that he was headed for *"a flourishing finish."* That's a man of faith. This should inspire us and speak to us. A mega outpouring is beginning to build. The keystone holding it all together is being raised and the Church, the remnant warriors, is headed for a flourishing finish. Your purpose and destiny is headed for a flourishing finish. You are cycling right now into your most productive period. You will now see birthed on this planet what we couldn't birth on our own. The divisions of angels sent by Holy Spirit are going to help us finish well. They are going to help us break up, break out, break through, pass over, and possess a glorious future. We are moving forward from a literal Pentecost into surge after surge of replenishing outpourings from Heaven. The remnant will be soaked with power from on high. Our greatest days are in front of us!

Prayer

Father, You have the final say. Yours is the victory! I align my heart with this truth today. We will break out and break through!

84

TIME TO PUSH

We decree "now be" to the promises of God.

Holy Spirit has been preparing us for a battle for this nation. The drums of spiritual, cultural, and moral wars are beating. The battle lines have been drawn. On one side is the true Church, the people of God, and concerned citizens who have not been radicalized by hell's ideologies. On the other side are radicalized soldiers of senseless ideologies, those whose minds are filled with nonsense, some of whom are bullies for Baal. They are bullies like Goliath who are defying the Living God and His Word. They are defiant against Christianity. That defiance is now at a fever pitch, and it's our turn to answer the call. Answer it we must and answer it we will. The discordant sounds of Goliath will not chill us. Rather, they will inspire us to make a stand.

The context of this moment is important to note. The Godhead has prepared us very well. We have moved into the most supernatural era Holy Spirit has ever led. The wonder of that statement is difficult to even fathom because there have definitely been many supernatural eras down through history when mind-blowing miracles took place. Holy Spirit also said, "The greatest harvest of souls ever will occur in this era." The prophets have declared a billion-soul harvest and the greatest revival and outpouring of power there has ever been.

This outpouring will affect every mountain of the culture. It will affect the governments of nations. It will inspire miraculous change, and it will cause a supernatural reset.

I know of no other era with this amount of angelic assistance. The angels are here to harken to the Word of God that the Ekklesia decrees, according to Psalm 103:20. We are in a God-planned moment. The future before us is Holy Spirit's most supernatural era.

There are prophetic words and promises that have been given to the Ekklesia that are now to unfold. We are being called to travail and pray birthing prayers for them, just as the prophet Elijah did.

After three and a half years of drought, God told Elijah it was time for rain. He told him to declare it to Ahab. Elijah did, and after declaring it's time for rain, he began to pray for rain. He prayed seven times, kneeling in the way that Israeli women assumed when birthing their children. He prayed birthing and travailing prayers because it was due. The water had broken on a promise, and it was time to deliver it. It was time to push with pushing prayer. There are prophetic words now in their moment. The contractions have begun, and it's time to push.

We must understand prophetic words or promises of Scripture are not automatic; they are conditional to our response. We must agree and decree. We must speak our faith and pray them to come to pass. We must speak "now be" to promises.

For 25 years, Abraham and Sarah stewarded the promise from God that they would have a son. When Abraham was 99 years old, he shifted into *now* faith rather than just hoping that it would someday happen. He began to call what was not as though it was. He began to say out loud and declare in the atmosphere for Isaac to come to him, literally declaring, "Isaac, come; come here, son; come to me." Holy Spirit is calling the Ekklesia to pray "come here" prayers. Come here, promises. Come here, prophetic words. Come here, dreams. Come here, visions. Come here.

Prayer

Holy Spirit, to every promise You've spoken and every purpose You've uttered, we say, "Come here and come here now, in Jesus' Name."

85

Authority Language

We decree the Ekklesia is speaking the King's language. We are speaking with authority.

The best example that we have for speaking authority language is, of course, Jesus Himself. John 7:46 (NKJV) says concerning Jesus, *"No man ever spoke like this Man!"* Matthew 7:28-29 (KJV) says, *"...people were astonished at his doctrine: for he taught them as one having authority...."* In other words, He spoke differently. His language was powerful and His words were weighty. Jesus' sentences were not filled with unbelief. He didn't contradict Himself, saying one thing one minute and something else the next. His speech was not confusing. His words were positive, sure, decisive, confident, and bold. Jesus spoke kingly language. For example, He didn't say to the leper who came asking to be made clean, "I'm not really feeling it today, but I guess I could try." No, He spoke with authority.

In Luke 7, Jesus approached a widow woman who had just lost her only son and was leading a funeral procession right toward Him. Rather than just getting out of the way and letting death walk right by Him, He confronted the situation as Holy Spirit led Him. He spoke with authority to the young man, "Rise," and he got up.

In John 9, Jesus didn't tell a man who was born blind, "Blindness is too hard for Me to heal." No, He spoke with authority, and vision came into those blind eyes. In John 11, Jesus didn't tell Lazarus' sisters, Mary and Martha, "Sorry about your brother, but there's nothing I can do. He's been in the grave way too long." No, compassion and the energy of Holy Spirit rose inside Him; and when it did, He spoke with bold authority, "Lazarus, come forth," and he came back to life.

Absolutely no one spoke with more authority than Jesus. He exemplified to His joint heirs the importance of using authority language. Luke the physician writes in Luke 4:32 (KJV), *"They were astonished at his doctrine: for his word was with power."* The Amplified Bible, Classic Edition says, *"They were amazed at His teaching, for His word was with authority and ability and weight and power."*

Jesus talked as though He was authorized. He used His words to influence. The words of our King were forceful. He spoke like a potentate. He spoke like a magistrate who knew His jurisdiction. He spoke with power. His words were sure and spoken with might.

Our King spoke against demon powers and ruled over them. He gave commands to demons. He didn't take commands. He activated His authority with His words, and like a master magistrate He told devils to go and they did. Shouldn't we do likewise? Shouldn't His Church do likewise? Shouldn't His heirs' speech drip with authority? Are we not supposed to represent Him? Aren't we to do what He did?

Kings talk differently. Their speech resonates with authority. They carry themselves with authority. It's time for a remnant Bride to begin to carry herself with authority, knowing that a yes on earth is a yes in Heaven and a no on earth is a no in Heaven. Knowing that Heaven, Holy Spirit, and Angel Armies are backing it up.

PRAYER

Father, because we are joint heirs with Jesus, in His Name we rise to plant the heavens and the earth with faith decrees aligned with Your Word.

86

SUPERNATURAL CONFIDENCE

We decree the Kingdom of God will stand.

The first Ekklesia prayed for boldness to confront adversarial culture, government, religion, and ideologies (see Acts 4:29-30). So must we. We need a baptism, an anointing of boldness. We're not going to change this nation with passive, nominal, indifferent, scared, wimpy Christianity. We need unintimidated boldness.

I recently began to pray the same prayer the disciples did in Acts 4. After praying, "Lord, give us bold, fearless confidence to declare Your Word, to stand for You. Give us miracles, Lord. Give us signs. Give us wonders. Display visibly the power that is in the Name of Jesus," I then began to pray a very simple prayer. In this prayer, I simply said, "Holy Spirit, what are You saying right this minute, right this afternoon? What is our Kingdom doing at this precise moment? Jesus said in Revelation that we are to hear what You are saying, that You will tell us what's going on. What is going on at this moment?"

Usually when I pray those kinds of prayers, there is a time of seeking, knocking, and pursuing. This time, Holy Spirit answered immediately and there was a boldness in His voice that I instantly picked up on. He said:

> "We're preparing now to show the world the strength of the Lord of Hosts. He is tired of His sons and daughters being bullied.

> And now the strong arm of the Lord will be seen overpowering and defeating the forever loser through a functioning Ekklesia. For, know this, My Ekklesia will enter into times when prophetic words, promises, dreams, and visions will intersect their moment, activating the assignments I put in them. As My Ekklesia engages in prayer and in decrees, and corresponding actions functioning in My original intent, My original purpose for its being, it will connect to a supernatural moment that I have planned for revival and reformation. Strength will multiply. Doors will open. Changes will surge forward. Transformation of the times will come. Crooked paths will be made straight. Realignment to right ways will manifest. Restoration to paths of righteousness will be rebuilt. Move forward into My moment. Move forward into your moment. My move, your move. My word, your word. My victory, your victory. Engage with purpose into My moment. Engage the battle, says the Lord."

I believe we have been prepared for this moment. We must now be very bold and fearless. We cannot be passive onlookers. We must live in the fear of the Lord, not the fear of man. Like Shadrach, Meshach, and Abednego, and countless other heroes of faith, we must shake off all religious passivity and stand strong. No bowing to Baal. No bowing to wickedness, perversion, mutilators of children, demon doctrines, government intimidations, insane ideas, or demon propaganda. No bowing to lies to keep the peace. No bowing to any antichrist agenda.

We must embrace a Kingdom of God mentality. We must embrace the remnant warriors' mentality. Remnant warriors like David, like Gideon's three hundred. We must remove cowardice and religious passivity that is like leaven, polluting the whole thing. We must be filled with boldness.

The King says, "*Engage the battle now. Stand and fight the good fight of faith.*" I believe this is our moment to win decisive victories. Millions of prayers have filled the prayer bowls of Heaven. Millions of decrees have been made, and now we are seeing the assignments embedded into prophetic words begin to uproot, tear down, and plant new, just like God has said in seasons past.

PRAYER

Lord, give us bold, fearless confidence to declare Your Word, to stand for You. Holy Spirit, fill us with supernatural boldness to say what You are saying and step out in faith.

87

Decreeing to See

We decree that promises of God are coming into season. His promises are materializing now.

Decrees create. They can create ideas in your heart. They create things that are not seen with the natural eye. They can create changes in conditions and in the atmosphere physically, spiritually, emotionally, materially, governmentally, politically, vocationally, and provisionally. Decrees are a creative force, and they release a creative force that will bless us abundantly.

In Isaiah 42:9 (KJV), God says, "*...new things do I declare: before they spring forth I tell you of them.*" Notice that He says, "I declare them before they spring forth. I pronounce them before they ever are." Smith and Goodspeed's translation reads, "*New things I foretell—before they spring into being, I will announce them to you.*" So God says, "I announce them. I declare without negation first so that they can be seen."

The New Jerusalem Bible reads, "*Fresh things I now reveal; before they appear I tell you of them.*" The Knox Translation says, "*I tell you now what is still to be; you shall hear it before it ever comes to light.*" God says, "If it is to be, if I have purposed it to be, I will speak it first before it ever comes to life." First comes a decree—a declared word that He will not change or negate. The Living Bible reads, "*I will prophesy again. I will tell you the future before it happens.*" That's what prophecy is—foretelling something before it happens. Anyone can prophesy after something happens. God says, "I explain with My words what is to be before it ever is, and then it springs forth and materializes. It doesn't materialize until I speak it. It doesn't materialize until there's a decree." That's what Hebrews 11:1 is about—faith decreed becomes substantive. Faith-filled words materialize if you don't negate them.

The word *before* in Isaiah 42:9 is the Hebrew word *tehrem.* It is a very important word for believers and the Church to understand because it means "suspended in time or not yet occurred" (Strong's H2962). So God says, "While its existence is suspended in time, while it has not yet occurred, I decree it."

The two words *spring forth* are from one Hebrew word—*tsamach.* It is an agricultural word that means "to sprout, to bud, and to grow to fullness" (Strong's H6779). It indicates a process that will come to fullness, to maturity. It first sprouts, then buds, and finally it grows to fullness when it's decreed or planted. It will not come to fullness until it is decreed. The word *tell* is the Hebrew word *shama,* meaning "to sound a message, to announce something, to proclaim, or to voice" (Strong's H8085).

In order to create, you have to voice it. Before it occurs, announce it. While it is suspended in time, while it has not occurred yet, you have to announce it. It will never produce what it is if you don't plant it and decree it.

PRAYER

Lord Jesus, today I choose to partner with Heaven. I realign my heart and mind and will fill my mouth with faith-filled words.

88

WINNING WORDS

We decree we are triumphant, healed and victorious in Jesus' Name.

Romans 4:21 (KJV) says that Abraham became *"fully persuaded"* that what God had promised He was able to perform. *Fully persuaded* is the Greek phrase *plerophoreo,* meaning "to convince or win over with words" (Strong's G4135). God won Abraham over with His words. We could say that He spoke winning words to Abraham. Interestingly, it has an implied reciprocity in the Greek language. In other words, when Abraham spoke winning words to God, planting them in the heavens, God spoke winning words back to him. Abraham declared, "I win," and God echoed it from Heaven, "Yes, you win."

Thankfully, God never speaks to us with words of condemnation. He doesn't call us losers. He doesn't say to us, "You can't make it. You are now going to fail. You're a failure. You're going to be overcome." No, it's *plerophoreo.* When you believe what God says and you decree it, God says you win. You are a winner. You're an overcomer. You will now succeed.

When you put faith in the promise of God, God begins to speak winning words to you. Winning words begin to rise up in your spirit against the negative words of your mind. The winning words of God in your spirit begin to overcome, and you begin to win and succeed. God speaks winning words to you. He says, "You are a winner. You cannot lose. You are a champion. You are a conqueror. You're victorious. You're triumphant. You're an overcomer. You are going to make it. You are going to get this done. You are an achiever." We are to echo back to Him in agreement, "I am a winner. I can't lose. I'm a champion. I'm an overcomer. I'm victorious. I'm triumphant. I'm healed. I'm an overcomer. I'm going to make it. I can do it. I will achieve this goal. I will get this done. Miracles are materializing for me."

Many today have promises suspended in time that haven't occurred yet, but we are to say to them, "Come here," and not negate it. If the people of God would dare to do what He said and begin to declare "Come here," we would see great creative promises begin to spring up all over the place. But so often negative words come to our minds and go out of our mouths, surround our necks, and strangle the life out of our faith. Don't do it. We are to refuse to look at the conditions. If you look at the conditions, you are going to get very discouraged. You could look at the condition of our nation and get very discouraged. Instead, look at God. Observe what He says and all the promises He has made to us.

These are the greatest days in church history. When are we going to declare that? Ponder His ability to perform His promise. Rise in authority language and bid promises *come here, come here, come here*. If you want to see promises sprout, bud, and grow to fullness, get hold of the principles of faith (not just in a knowing way but in a doing way). It's amazing to me how many people know what faith is and yet don't do it. Choose today to activate your faith and say, "I am going to do it, and I am going to see the promises of God materialize in my life. I am declaring, *come here, come here, come here*."

Prayer

King Jesus, You speak words of life over me, so I choose to speak life too. Open my ears to hear what You are saying so I can partner my heart with Yours.

89

Light Brigade

We decree the Ekklesia is standing for the cause. We won't back down.

Our commission is not unclear. We know exactly what our King has ordered. The light of the world has stepped into darkness to illuminate it with the glory of God's radiant redemption, to light it with God's good news of the Gospel of Jesus Christ. The King is looking for another "Light Brigade." The King is looking for those who will shine His light, those who will reign in this life and reign with His authority, those who will ride in the Name of Jesus. Those who, empowered by our Kingdom, filled with the mightiness of Holy Spirit, will ride into the jaws of hell and they won't back up. They will ride and take back the inheritance and bring back what the enemy has stolen.

I have gone all over most of the counties of Ohio for the cause. I don't get paid to do it. I just do it for the cause. I went through a very intense battle a few years ago when I was attacked with Bell's palsy after a ministry time. I went through six weeks of vertigo. I would sit in the front row of the church and they would tape my sagging cheek up, with a small microphone taped to it, because I refused to let this stop me from speaking. I couldn't walk around because of the vertigo, so I just clung to the podium while I spoke because the cause is worth it. My King is worth it. Everything about Him is worth it to me. You can't let satan win!

Many weeks later, I was lying on a seat in the back of a bus around 2:00 a.m. I began to think, *Is this worth it? What can I do? I believe one guy can do something, but am I fooling myself? Is what I'm doing meaningful?* I just laid back there, feeling awful, when an old story came to mind. I knew it was the Holy Spirit prompting.

I remembered the story of a kid who was out on the beach in Florida early in the morning and a rogue wave had pushed in all kinds of crabs, washing thousands of them onto the shore. This little kid is out there grabbing the crabs and throwing them back in the water. Along comes an old guy—you know how some are, with their silly hats and 40-year-old shorts—and he stops and watches the kid. Finally he asks, "Son, what are you doing?" The boys answers, "The waves pushed all the crabs up here on the shore and I'm throwing them back." The old guy looks around at all the thousands of crabs up and down the beach and he says, "Well, son, you think what you're doing matters?" The little kid picks up another crab, throws it into the sea, and says, "It matters to that one."

Who can you touch? It matters. The King can synergize that together. Do something that matters. Answer His call. It's time to make a stand. I'm not talking about something grandiose. You may not be able to throw them all back, but make your stand. Do something that matters for King Jesus. Do it. Do it. Do it.

PRAYER

Deep calls to deep inside, Lord. I ask that You speak deep inside of me. What can I do to make a difference? How can I make a wild charge for You?

90

MINISTERING SPIRITS

We decree supernatural help is rising and angelic help is here.

Several years ago, Holy Spirit began to talk to me concerning the function of the seraphim order of angels. I believe He did that in preparation for the connection of a time and place for supernatural reformation. Holy Spirit uses seraphim and other angel orders in assisting the heirs of God and the Ekklesia to accomplish Godhead surprises and massive transitions in the earth realm. Hebrews 1:14 (KJV) says this concerning angels: *"Are they not all ministering spirits, sent forth to minister for them who shall be heirs of salvation?"* That would be us, the Church; we are the heirs of salvation.

Government angels assist the Ekklesia's administrative authority. When we make governing decrees, this order of angels aids in their coming to pass. They are essential in assisting the Ekklesia in the binding and loosing of things, as stated in Matthew 16:19.

Awakening and reformation angels, like the angels of fire that Holy Spirit had with Him on the day of Pentecost in Acts 2, assist in outpourings, revivals, and fresh Pentecost in our times. Holy Spirit once told me that the same angels that accompanied Him on the day of Pentecost are also available to assist us today in new Pentecost outpourings. I didn't share this with anyone for quite some time because of what people might think. Sadly, neither the reality nor the release of angels has been properly understood because some churches have minimized their existence. For whatever reason, they have emphasized the work of demons, but not of angels. That has never made sense to me.

Why wouldn't we believe what God's Word says? If we're going to be part of supernatural reformation, we're going to have to believe in the supernatural in the earth realm. We see this clearly in the precedents at the birth of Jesus: the spirit realm was involved. Angels, miracles, and signs in the heavens were involved. Someday, there's going to be another sign in the heavens and people are going to know Almighty God is coming in a different measure.

Seraphs are also working and protecting the altars of the Ekklesia. You will recall the seraph in Isaiah 6 who flew to an altar and took a red-hot glowing coal with a pair of tongs, which he touched to Isaiah's lips to cleanse Isaiah's lips to speak purely. In Isaiah 6, God had asked this question, *"Who can I send, who will go for Us?"* Isaiah had answered him, *"Here am I, Lord, send me."* Then the seraph ministered fire to cleanse the message, assisting in preparing the messenger to be sent. I see this happening in the coming years, as the heirs are being prepared for assignments and callings. Angels are assisting Holy Spirit's calling to fire up the remnant and the saints, to be sent forth with great power and with fiery passion.

The Lord gave me a word at our Prophetic Summit recently. Here is part of that word regarding angelic help:

> "My seraphs will proclaim messages from the Godhead. Do not be surprised by this. Expect this. They will assist the bringing to pass of prophetic words that are now at full term. There are some at full term. They will battle the delay tactics of the forever loser. Supernatural reformation will amp up and roll through the earth as Heaven's King and His Kingdom take center stage. He will not be upstaged by fools. His Church will prevail. The earth will shake. Everything that can be shaken will. His Kingdom will not. You will not."

PRAYER

Lord, let Your glory come and fill Your Ekklesia with a fiery message—to make known who You are to a watching world. We open our hearts to You now. Purify us, King of Glory!

91

WORDS OF LIFE

We decree that our words are filled with life and our words will create.

The Scriptures teach very clearly and powerfully that God wants His sons and daughters living out their lives on earth with great purpose and meaning. He desires for His heirs to live with a sense of destiny, peace, and joy, knowing that goals set before them can be reached. His laws of life and the Dominion Mandate that He has given from Genesis 1 will work for us. It will work for any born-again believer if it is applied. No one is exempt. Word seeds will grow and produce for us. Authority language will work for us, and our lives will experience the results.

As far as God is concerned, your future is very bright. Your life is to be lived out in a very good, peaceful, gracious way. Your destiny is good. There are no disasters planned for you. His plans for you are good and hope-filled. Your potential is absolutely awesome.

From the very beginning in Genesis 1, God has designed it so that the potential He has placed inside of all of us is activated by the words of faith we speak and by actions of obedience in line with what God says. There is so much potential in the world today. You are loaded with potential. Potent power is in you to be something you've never been before or do something you've never done before.

Word seed decrees will help create your future. Your words are seeds that produce after their kind. Destiny words, along with words of success and purpose, can grow to fullness when believed and acted upon. They prod you to produce. They germinate, grow, and reproduce themselves.

As born-again believers, we know that when we stand before God we will give an account for certain actions. I don't think many understand that we will also give an account for the words we speak. This leads us to a word that we need to understand—*idle*. Here, it is the Greek word *argos*—a particle of negation. *Idle* or *argos* in the Greek language means "inactive, unemployed, useless, barren, nonworking, and unprofitable" (Strong's G692). It would mean *not* active, *not* working, *not* profitable. Jesus said we will answer for useless, negative, or idle words too.

Idle words cause promises to be nonworking and inactive in us. Negative words are unprofitable. Notice that Jesus said if there are negative thoughts in the heart, they will proceed from your mouth. Negative thoughts are going to come out of your mouth and cause promises to become barren. *Argos* does not produce abundant life; it produces un-life, not-life, or un-fulfillment. It produces un-success, empty desires. Negative words bring about a forfeiture of benefits.

In Matthew 12:37 (NKJV), Jesus also says, *"For by your words you will be justified, and by your words you will be condemned." Justified* is the Greek word *dikaioo*, and it means "to set forth as righteous because of receiving Christ's payment for sins" (Strong's G1344). Born-again believers are made to be righteous because of the shed blood of Jesus and Calvary. We are made to be righteous and are due certain rights because we are now heirs—heirs of God and joint heirs with Christ.

PRAYER

God, I repent of any words spoken that have been a curse instead of a blessing. Make me aware of the words of my mouth so that I can partner with what Heaven decrees.

92

Nail Down

We decree God's words are in our minds and in our mouths.

God's words are always right words. When we meditate upon God's Word, when we roll it around and around in our minds until we are renewed by what He says, it begins to penetrate our hearts and our spirits. God's Word leaves an impression. It leaves its seal in us. Then out of our hearts, Jesus said, our mouths speak and agree with the impression God's Word has left there.

The right words will press our problems to conform to the promises that are in our hearts. The right words will be forcible and change situations, activating the promises of God and stamping the seal of God's promise on the problem. The idea is to press the problems to conform to God's Word by declaring your faith. Right words carry the weight of the Kingdom of Almighty God behind them.

In Ecclesiastes 12:11 (KJV), the aging King Solomon wrote, *"The words of the wise are as goads."* A goad was a long stick that was sharpened to a point like a spear, and they would use this goad to make their oxen or cattle move. Today, they use electric cattle prods. Solomon said that the words of the wise are like that. Their words keep them moving toward their purpose, goals, and success. Their words keep them from standing still and becoming stagnant. Their words keep producing for them. Their words prod them forward and onward, steadily plowing through to victory.

Solomon also says in Ecclesiastes 12:11 (KJV) the words of the wise are *"as nails fastened by the masters of assemblies."* We would call them master carpenters or builders today. A master carpenter knows where to nail something together. He makes his nails work for him. Solomon said that's what a wise person does with words—nails down the promise of God with words. He makes words work for him. Just like nails are used to hold boards in place, words are used to hold promises in place. Nail down God's answer for your problems with the words of your mouth. Decrees are your nails. They nail God's promise in place. Nail your adversary, your opposition, and the situation. Nail it with God's Word, with the promise of the Living God.

Wise King Solomon also wrote in Proverbs 6:2 (KJV), *"Thou art snared with the words of thy mouth, thou art taken with the words of thy mouth."* The two words *snared* and *taken* have similar Hebrew meanings—"to be caught in a trap and captured" (Strong's H3369, H3920). They literally mean to become a prisoner of war. Wrong words can snare you, causing you to become a prisoner of war, bound up, ineffective, unable to move as you want. Wrong words allow demon traps to snare you. Your words can either work for you or against you; they'll either nail down the promise of God for your life, or you're the one who will get nailed.

Wise people use their words like a master carpenter and make their words work for them. Their words become like well-driven nails that build a strong and secure house. They use their words to build life into themselves and into their family. They use their words to create a blessed world to live in. Your words are indeed forcible.

PRAYER

Holy Spirit, as You build with Your words, teach us to do the same with our words. Show us where to speak and who to speak to. Give us wisdom as we speak, each word a step toward victory in You.

93

KING BREAKER

We decree break up. Break out. Break through. Pass over. Possess.

The Breaker Himself and His Holy Spirit have plans, and His angels are being activated and are going forth into this world to break up, break out, break through. They are enabling us to pass over and possess our inheritance. They are being released by the millions upon this planet to assist us in awesome breakthrough.

It is our time to break out and pass over into an inheritance in new ways at new levels. We've come into a fullness of time—meaning prophetic words, dreams, and visions are now connecting to their moment. Our prayers are hitting the mark; they have been heard, and Heaven is answering. The Ekklesia is being seated with an anointing to prevail. They are being seated with Christ's authority, declared from their lips at levels the world has never seen before. There is boldness and their decrees of faith are being heard, activating and permitting some things on earth and deactivating or forbidding others. We're entering seasons of supernatural breakthrough. They will happen in your life and in churches everywhere.

> The One who breaks open the way will go up before them; they will break through the gate and go out. Their King will pass through before them, the Lord at their head (Micah 2:13 NIV).

Please notice King Jesus is identified as King Breaker who goes before us to ensure our breakthrough. He leads us through *gates,* which is the Hebrew word *shaar*, which means "doors" (Strong's H8179). Doors to new areas, opportunities, places, or lands. It represents a way through.

Jesus is the Way Opener. He goes before His people to break up obstacles, opening the way to new promised territories, inheritance, and destiny (both individual and corporate). The One who plans your destiny goes before you, breaking you free from any hinderance to that destiny.

The word *breaker* is the Hebrew word *parats* and it means "to break out, to burst out, to grow out, to grow through something" (Strong's H6555). It's like a seed that grows up out of the dirt and, as it does, it will break out and produce what it is. It's similar to a child who grows out of his/her clothes. This kind of breakthrough comes as a result of growth. You grow up and out.

Also, *parats* means "to increase in spiritual strength" until you're strong enough to break something. *Parats* means "the one who breaks up, goes before to give you strength to breakthrough." Breakthrough is the Hebrew word *abar* and it means "to pass over or to cross over" (Strong's H5674). According to Hebrew scholar Spiros Zodhiates, *parats* can also mean to impregnate with concepts, ideas, or purposes. *Parats* means the seed is planted and it goes through the growth process. It is nourished in the womb, then it breaks out of the womb and passes through to new life in the world, where it can grow and become who or what it is.

Prayer

King Jesus, You go before us. What shall we fear? You open the way and break up anything that stands as a barrier. Thank You. We will follow! We say yes!

94
It's Time

We decree the Greater One abides in us and we will move and operate in Your authority. We will overcome!

It's time to do some thinking. It's time to ponder some things about life—our involvement in it, why we are here, and what we are to do. It's time to use our brains and think on ways to fan the flames of reformation in the land. It's time to stand wisely for our King. It's time to shake off the fog of ambiguity and raise our voices in the United States of America again. The Church must become the conscience of this nation. This is the era, Holy Spirit is saying to the Church to begin the movement, make the stand, and become the conscience of your nation again.

Men and women have died for trivial causes and they have done it unashamedly. Many have died for illegal and immoral causes and they have done that unashamedly. Some have died for the cause of sin and its bondage. How much more should we, who serve the highest cause in all of time and eternity, look this world in the eye and say, "We stand and we back a cause." How much more should we stand up in front of a godless society and say, "We stand for the cause of Christ." How much more should we, the people of the living God, say in the face of hell itself, "We stand for the cause of Christ and we will no longer ignore your challenge."

It is time we say we are not going to be defied and ignore this lack of civility any longer. We will not be intimidated into silence. We will come alongside our standing King; and with His fresh outpouring, we are going to make a stand with the power of the Holy Spirit activating all the previous outpourings and anointings of history into our present time. We are going to make a prayer stand like has never been made before on this planet. Yes, we are going to appeal to Heaven. We will declare and we will stand for truth no matter who likes it. We will declare what God says regardless of whether the Supreme Court, media, government, or anybody else likes it.

We will not be ashamed of the Gospel of Jesus Christ. We will not be reticent. We will not just stay out of things. We are going to get into everything. We're not going to stay out of the elections, government, or education. It's time we showed this world we do not take our orders from you. We take our orders from King Jesus.

Our Kingdom and our nation does not need more bystanders. We need unintimidated warriors standing for the cause. When the King of kings returns and I have to stand before Him, as all of us will, and give an account for what I did in this life, I do not want to hear Him say, "I gave you authority. I gave you power. I gave you Angel Armies. I gave you all the coalition forces of Heaven to back you up. Why didn't you do something?" It's time to make our stand.

PRAYER

Lord, Your Bride will stand with You. I will stand with You. My words will stand with You. My heart will stand with You. We appeal to Heaven, come in increasing measure. May hearts everywhere be drawn toward righteousness.

95

GOVERNING AUTHORITY

We decree we have the keys and we will win in Jesus' Name!

The government of the Kingdom of God is now on the shoulders of King Jesus. All authority has been given to Him in Heaven and on earth. He has the keys to every door. He can open the doors or close them. Now, amazingly, Heaven's King and the King of our Kingdom, Jesus, says in Matthew 16:19 that He's giving His Ekklesia access to all the keys. That is incredible. In essence He said, "In My Name, My Ekklesia can now bind. It can loose. It can open. It can close. It can forbid or permit. In My Name I am giving My joint heirs access to all the keys. They can declare doors to open. They can declare them to close. I'm putting the keys of governing authority in their hands."

Hear what He is saying. Listen with spiritual ears. Let the truth of this take root, and dare to believe the One who cannot lie. That is who is talking—the Word made flesh. The One who speaks and what He speaks is infused with His authority. In other words, He has the right to say this. If He wants to give you the keys, He has the right to do it. There is no issue. If He wants to give you the keys to everything, He can.

> This is the rock on which I will put together my church, a church so expansive with energy that not even the gates of hell will be able to keep it out. And that's not all. You will have complete and

> free access to God's kingdom, keys to open any and every door: no more barriers between heaven and earth, earth and heaven. A yes on earth is yes in heaven. A no on earth is no in heaven (Matthew 16:18-19 MSG).

One of the most vital of those keys is the baptism of the Holy Spirit and His gift of praying in Spirit language. It's so vital that this King, who made this promise, also says, "Don't even try it until Holy Spirit fills you and reactivates government language. Don't even attempt it without Him. You won't get it done without Holy Spirit." For more than 2,000 years the Church, for the most part, didn't even think about it. But something is happening. A remnant is rising and implementing Spirit-governing language and loosing governing intercession in the Spirit.

If you need access to the Judge, you have a key. Pray it in the Spirit. If you need access to the King's treasury, you have an access key. Let Holy Spirit fill you and use your Spirit language. Need to petition the court of Heaven for a ruling in your favor? One vital key is praying in other tongues as the Spirit gives the utterance. Need a door opened? Need one closed? You have a key. Pray it in the Spirit.

PRAYER

Holy Spirit, may Your presence come now to bring forth fresh utterances of Your intercession in my heart. Open our spiritual eyes and ears. Fill our mouths. Show us the keys.

96

LOGOS TO RHEMA

We decree the rhema word of God is coming now to bring clarity, hope, peace and life in Jesus' Name.

Rhema means a word that God speaks "fresh" to us. *Rhema* is a personalized word, anointed and spoken to us personally. It's a word of promise that Holy Spirit breathes fresh anointing on, causing it to come alive to us. It's not just a general word out of the Scriptures that we have read. *Rhema* is Holy Spirit-made-alive words given to you personally by God and anointed to speak to you. In other words, you have a knowing inside you that this is your word and you know it. God is saying this to *you*. This word is alive in *you*. This word has God's breath on it. It has been breathed into *you*, and it's living inside of *you*.

If you have ever been reading the Bible and, all of a sudden, a certain phrase or a certain sentence just comes alive, that is *rhema*. Holy Spirit has activated a thought or a principle or a promise to you. It's no longer general knowledge that you have been reading. It's God speaking it directly to *you*.

When we are reading the Bible, God's written Word, we are reading what is called the *logos*, meaning the general information God wants you to know. We are to read the Bible for that information, but it's not *rhema* until Holy Spirit makes what we are reading come alive to us.

Logos is just information; *rhema* is revelation. It's not *rhema* until He breathes fresh life in it and you know—this is for *me*, this is *mine*.

That's why it is important to meditate on God's Word. You have to ponder it and cast in your mind what it means. Think on it, pray about its meaning to you. We have to spend time in His presence allowing time for Him to quicken or make alive His promise and His Word to us. Spend time in communion with the Holy Spirit, giving Him the opportunity to breathe upon that word inside.

Sometimes people try to claim a promise that they've read and they wonder why it's not working so well. One of the reasons could be they haven't spent time with the Holy Spirit, allowing Him to incubate into their spirit and "life" it into their hearts. Here is the principle—it's relational. You don't seek promises. You seek *Him* until He gives you a promise. You seek *Him* until He breathes on that promise.

This is about relationship and activated faith is required. You have to meditate on a promise from the Word of God or a prophecy until you know that you know Holy Spirit is breathing life into that inside you. Just like He breathed life into man in the beginning, His breath does the same to His Word, to the *logos* that you have been studying. It's made alive—this is *your* promise, *your* word.

PRAYER

Lord, breathe life, principles, and promise into us today. Holy Spirit, breathe life into the hearts of Your people that will cause miracles to begin to grow to fullness, miracles that have been grabbed hold of that will become potent. Let Your breath breathe on promises inside our hearts, Lord.

97

Seeing the Impossible

We decree our eyes will see what You see, God. Our ears will hear what You hear. Promises of God, come here now.

In Genesis 12:2-3, God told a man named Abraham—Abram at the time—that he was going to be the heir of the world and the father of nations. Notice that this was before Abram ever had a son, and God decreed this to Abram when it was impossible for him. Abram was 99 years old and Sarah—Sarai at the time—was 89 years old, well past the age to bear children. But God isn't bound to any limitations. He wasn't bothered by what Sarah and Abraham looked like or their age. It didn't matter.

While having a child was suspended in time and before it occurred (*tehrem*), God prophesied it. While it looked impossible, God announced it. He declared it. He spoke authority words of faith. He created what was humanly impossible with His words. You must decree words of faith first in order to create promises that are impossible where humans are concerned. You must declare what seems impossible in the natural realm to see it materialize. Then it can spring forth, sprout, bud, and grow to fullness.

The promise will remain impossible, suspended in time, until it's decreed. The moment it's decreed, it becomes possible. When the promise is decreed, it is conceived—it goes past mere knowledge and becomes substance that is planted and can grow.

Romans 4:17 (KJV) says, *"(As it is written, I have made thee the father of many nations,) before him whom he believed, even God, who quickeneth the dead, and calleth those things which be not as though they were."* That is one of the most loaded statements in all of Scripture. Understanding it is of paramount importance to moving in faith and creating things that don't exist with your words. God's declaration was, *"I have made you a father of many nations"* (Genesis 17:5 NKJV). It is done. You are a father. There is no ambiguity in that statement. There is no "maybe" and nothing negative injected into it. God went so far as to change his name from Abram to Abraham because Abraham means *"father of a multitude"* (Genesis 17:5 AMP). God decreed what He expected to see, even though it looked impossible to man.

The principle is very clear—we are to decree what we expect to see, using authority language. We have to live like who we truly are—the sons and daughters of God. Much of the Church is passive where their faith is concerned, waiting to see something before they decree something. But, you cannot see if you don't decree. It's just not possible.

The principle is clear in the lives of Old Testament saints as well as New Testament saints. It is also clear in the life of our King Jesus. If you want to see promises materialize, you have to decree them without negation. You must declare them *done* in His name.

Romans 4:17 (KJV) reads, *"God...calleth those things which be not as though they were."* The New English Translation reads, *"God who makes the dead alive and summons the things that do not yet exist as though they already do."*

We must use kingly language toward nonexistent things or things that must be changed. In Jesus' Name, we are to boldly decree—to things that are suspended in time, to promises that have not been fulfilled yet, to prophecy that has not occurred yet—"Come here and manifest to me."

PRAYER

Holy Spirit, when You see the promise and I fail to do so, bring clarity to me. Help me see as You see and decree until the impossibilities around me bend their knee to You.

98

THE GOD OF BREAKTHROUGH

We decree everything in the Kingdom of God is accelerating.

Hear the word of the Lord for this hour:

"It is time for the surge of My Kingdom. I will now rise and lead My people through gates of awesome breakthrough. I will break all confinements. Hear the sound of confinement breaking. Hear the sound of angels of breakthrough scattering and shattering confinement at My command. Economic, government, religious, and demonic confinement, break.

"For the forces of My Kingdom have been prepared to initiate the advance, and My angels have heard the command—begin the advance, remove the obstacles, and open the glory roads for the advance.

"My Holy Spirit has prepared strategies and is now moving Angel Army divisions to the battle. My Ekklesia has been aligned. I have tuned the voice of My apostles and prophets. I am leading the advance of My Kingdom. I have never led a retreat, a defeat, or a stalemate. I lead advances, victories, and deliverance. I am rising to lead My Kingdom in the magnificent advance that is promised. I am standing to lead the breakout.

"Hell's kingdom will now experience might it cannot withstand. Overwhelming force will now come to bear upon diabolical structures of darkness. Evil and deep-rooted iniquity will be uprooted by My advancing Kingdom. Warrior champions are rising to follow Me in unrelenting purpose, aggressive faith, and bold declarations. The world has not experienced aggressive power like I will now release through My remnant.

"For the generational winds are blowing in synergy. They are driving My march to change history. Evil empires will crumble. Evil structures will fall. Evil philosophies will be destroyed by truth. Evil roots deep within this nation will be exposed and destroyed by the faith decrees of My Kingdom.

"Hear the sound of Heaven. Hear the sound of fresh winds of Pentecost. Hear the sound of marching. Hear the sound of shoutings from radical remnant faith warriors. Hear the drums of the conquering King beginning to beat. Their resounding message is now resonating in the core of My remnant.

"My Holy Spirit is stirring their hearts with My heart. They will now press with Me into supernatural breakthrough. Miraculous turnarounds and explosive change will now break through. Bondage will suddenly break, and brand-new life and freedom will witness that My liberating force has come through their doors.

"Yes, I am rewriting the story of the downcast, bruised, forsaken, wounded, and the captives. Their witness of Me shall be My declaration through the ages. I am the Lord mighty to save. I am the Breaker. I am the God of Breakthrough. I will now rewrite your story. I will now rewrite the story of this nation. I will march when I want to march. I will go wherever I want to go, and I will do whatever I want to do.

"The attempt of the forever loser and his kingdom to resist Me will be futile. I have set My face and I will not relent. My remnant and Ekklesia will break through. Strongholds of hell will scatter and shatter. Glory that dispels darkness will shine. Do not faint, quit, turn back, or become passive. Advance with Me and My Kingdom. Advance under Holy Spirit anointings. Advance with My Angel Armies. Enter, by faith, the new season of breakthrough and you will birth breakthrough after breakthrough after breakthrough."

PRAYER

King Jesus, You are the Breaker, the One who sets everything right. Come in Your power to uproot and demolish every tactic of evil. We cry out for Your glory to come.

99
WINDS OF CHANGE

We decree we are going from glory to glory to glory.

Holy Spirit's word continues:

"Listen and you will hear the sound of awesome winds of change. Four quarter winds of change are blowing. For I have heard the cries of 'how long,' I have heard the cries against delays. You shall surely now enter your due season. My appointed time has come. My winds are shifting conditions in your favor. My power is shaking the heavens and the earth. Know that the great shaking will result in your favor.

"It is a shaking that shakes doors open, reveals hidden riches, and uncovers your inheritance. It is a shaking that breaks chains of bondage, setting you free. You will be free. I will break you free. You will now see the change that I have planned. Look for it and step forward into it. You will now see the change from wilderness wandering to awesome times of transitions into promised places, times, and dreams of your heart. Your conditions will change as you transition into abundance.

"My winds of change will blow upon My remnant. They will blow upon My Church. Miraculous change will be seen manifesting to displace barrenness. I am ending the barren times of My people. I am ending the dark, barren times hell has propagated against My Church. I am releasing the fresh winds of a new Pentecost, and that wind will blow darkness away. It will blow away the barren times, the strategies of darkness, and obstacles to My blessings. It will blow down the obstacles to cultural, academic, government resistance, and deceitful barricades of humanism and lawless propaganda will fall. It will blow down the antichrist activism meant to harass you.

"I am sending the winds of change. Lift up your eyes and look with expectancy. Lift up your voice and declare with expectancy. Lift up your hands and worship with expectancy. I am changing the season. I am sending transformation winds. I am soaking you with favor. I am freeing you to rise up with wings like eagles and soar on Holy Spirit winds. I am freeing you to run and not grow weary, to walk and not faint. I am empowering you to pass through the floods and not be harmed, to pass through the fire and not be burned.

"You will now enter the calving season of hopes, dreams, and confessions of faith. Let your heart embrace it. Let your soul embrace it. Let your mind embrace it. Miraculous winds of transformation are now blowing. Holy Spirit's anointing is being poured forth and the divisions of angel armies are coming to assist you."

Prayer

Holy Spirit, may Your winds of change come. We believe Your greatest days are here, even now. Show us the miraculous, release Your healing and wholeness upon the earth. Come, King of Heaven.

100

THE GREATEST DAYS

We decree the glory of the Lord is rising in far greater measure and the King's Ekklesias are bursting forth in His supernatural, transitional, and reformational power.

"I will now lead the most supernatural era I have ever led." Holy Spirit spoke these words to me at the end of 2023. He spoke them with such boldness and conviction that I trembled inside. I had no doubt it would happen.

The wonder of His statement is difficult to fathom. Most certainly there have been many supernatural eras throughout the centuries when mind-blowing miracles took place. But now He is saying there will be more signs, wonders, and miracles, notable miracles, in this era than any other. What hope that gives for our times! Millions of prayers have filled the prayer bowl of Heaven, ready to be poured out and answered. Millions of decrees of faith have been spoken and declared, planting the heavens. As Job 22:28 describes, they are being established.

Yes, we have moved into a supernatural era. Prophetic words are connecting to their moment—a billion-soul harvest, the greatest worldwide revival ever known, and the greatest outpourings of Holy Spirit power and refreshing. It will affect all flesh and miraculous changes will be seen in all nations.

This supernatural era includes the activation of Angel Armies at greater levels than have ever been seen. In previous books I have written about their ministry assistance to the Church and the heirs of God.

The divisions of angels are here to assist the enforcing of God's Word that we have believed and decreed. What powerful assistance the true Church is now receiving. We will prevail as Jesus promised. The Angel Armies are God enforcers sent in this most supernatural era at greater levels than we have ever experienced before.

Get ready for the greatest days in church history. They are not in our past; they are in our present and in our future. It is time to partner with Holy Spirit in this era. It is time to partner with His powerful enforcers. It is time to win great battles.

The glory of the Lord is rising in far greater measure than we've ever seen before. I want to do my part, whether it's big or small, to see this happen. I fully know that it is led by Holy Spirit. I can contend, and I can believe. I know it is part of His plan for this era, and we are going to see it happen.

It is part of His plan for the King's Ekklesia to loose Christ's healing power at levels never seen before. Holy Spirit has said to me this supernatural, transitional, reformational era has now begun. Hell will try to stop it, but it is being released. This era is going to be a supernatural era and part of that involves healing and miracles. Let us set our gaze on our King and contend for His glory to come.

Prayer

Holy Spirit, activate Your Angel Armies now to partner with Your Ekklesia. We cry out for a revival fire to sweep across our homes, families, and nations. Unleash new realms of Your glory. We ready ourselves for Your coming.

About Tim Sheets

Dr. Tim Sheets is an apostle, pastor, and author based in southwestern Ohio. As pastor/apostle of Oasis Church in Middletown, Ohio, he and his wife, Carol, host many national events including an annual Prophetic Summit and quarterly Healing Summits. His vision is to raise up people who will authentically demonstrate the Church on earth and passionately evangelize the world. His heart is for awakening, revival, and reformation in America.

In the Right Hands, This Book Will Change Lives!

Most of the people who need this message will not be looking for this book. To change their lives, you need to **put a copy of this book in their hands.**

Our ministry is constantly seeking methods to find the people who need this anointed message to change their lives. **Will you help us reach these people?**

Extend this ministry by sowing 3 books, 5 books, 10 books, or more today, and become a life changer! Your generosity will be part of catalyzing the Great Awakening that many have been prophesying and praying for.